3

**MOST IMPORTANT STEPS
TO YOUR BETTER HEALTH
AND MIRACLE LIVING**

3

MOST IMPORTANT STEPS TO YOUR BETTER HEALTH AND MIRACLE LIVING

by Oral Roberts

ORAL ROBERTS ASSOCIATION

ISBN 0-8007-8313-1
Copyright © 1976 by Oral Roberts
Published by Fleming H. Revell Company

Printed in the United States of America

**Your life is God's gift to you.
What you do with your life
is your gift back to Him.**

Oral Roberts

A PERSONAL WORD FOR YOU

I am totally convinced of the healing power of prayer as a mighty instrument of God's healing for you. Nothing can shake me from this strong belief. When you know you are going to die and then something happens inside you and saves your life — that happened to me — that's convincing. I thank God for it.

But I'm also just as convinced that doctors and medicine are part of God's healing love to us. You see, I don't really care what instrument or delivery system God uses to bring healing and success — just so long as it comes. Right? I thank God for that.

Then, too, I've had to get myself by the bootstraps a few times and do something inside myself to get out of my own deadly negative emotions. And that's another one of God's instruments for healing — me improving my relationship with myself.

Can you imagine how I stood up and nearly shouted out loud when for the first time I really understood something Jesus said a long time ago ... I've been reading it for years ... I've preached on it ... but now listen to it!

> "Thou shalt love the Lord thy God with all thy heart, and with all thy soul, and with all thy strength, and with all thy mind; and thy neighbour as thyself" (Luke 10:27).

I've always thought of that as the love commandment, or "Golden Rule." It hadn't really dawned on me what He was saying until now.

He's telling you and me to get our relationships right:

1) our relationship with God.
2) our relationships with other people.
3) our relationship with ourself.

And the really exciting part of this is that it is powerful Seed-Faith working for my total healing and well-being.

For example:

When I know God as the Source of my total supply and look to Him for all my needs, *I've finally gotten into a right relationship with Him.*

When I'm reaching out to people and helping them find answers, and giving for the needs of others and learning to receive from God through others—that's the planting of precious seed to grow into the miracles I need. *And my relationship is right with others (my neighbor).*

When I get things straightened out inside me . . . when I'm confident and full of faith the way God told me to be and I'm expecting and receiving the miracles that are coming my way every day, *I've gotten into a right relationship with myself.*

Can you imagine how excited I am about this?

God is my Source—I look to Him.

I'll plant a seed—I reach out to others.

I'll expect a miracle—I'm getting what I need.

That's really how I got into Seed-Faith, to move my own mountain of need. I had to plant a seed out of that need—a seed to match my need. Then God said, "If you're really looking to Me as your Source, don't worry about mountains. Just be sure to plant the seed and I'll move the mountain." The seed will have in it the nature of an expanding force that breaks the mountain up and reduces it to a size you can deal with.

Talk about mountains being moved! It also included the hills that stood before me! I found I could face seriously ill people and give them a hope for God's healing. I found I could build a university, starting with nothing, even when the experts said it could not be done and I did it anyway, through God.

I have found I could go on nationwide television in prime time at a time when I was at the lowest of finances and when I thought my ministry was coming to a close.

What else would I find?

I found we were getting through to people. I found I could deal with a person with the most terrible problems you can imagine. sickness, spiritual, material, family, mental—you name it— and bring them into a position to receive a miracle.

I found I could combine God's healing instruments of prayer and medicine when everyone said it was not possible. I was even able to build a medical school that turns out not only skilled physicians, but also physicians who are filled with God's love for people.

What else have I found?

I have found I could face the stress and the anxiety of doing all these things and at the same time live in better health. I have even received a major healing within my own body by applying the principles of Seed-Faith—that is, giving and giving first.

Next, I found I couldn't wait to share these things with you. I wanted to put my arms around you and say, "*You can have better health. You can have success, and you can have it NOW.*"

That's when I got the idea to write this book, for I knew it wasn't enough to say, "You can have it." I knew I had to tell you *how* to have it.

God inside me is saying to you, "I know that I know that I know that I know that you can get your mountains to move. You can have the very desires of your heart. You can have success and get into miracle-living."

If you are ready, let's go!

Step Number

ONE

You will be in great position to have health and success *if* your relationship with God your Source is right.

AUTHOR'S NOTE:

Remember, be sure to read my Personal Word before you begin reading this book. My Personal Word will introduce you to how and why I wrote it.

Chapter 1   **page 33**

HOW YOU CAN RECEIVE THE GREATEST MIRACLE YOU CAN EVER HAVE

 key issue:

I Will Put First Things First

Chapter 2   **page 39**

HOW YOU CAN BECOME AWARE OF SIN IN YOUR LIFE

key issue:

I Am Aware Of My Need For A New Life

Chapter 3   **page 47**

IT'S NOT YOUR FAULT YOU ARE A SINNER, BUT IT IS IF YOU DON'T DO SOMETHING ABOUT IT

key issue:

I Am On The Road To A New Life And Better Health Because Of God My Source

Chapter 4   **page 59**

HOW TO KNOW YOU ARE BORN AGAIN REGARD-LESS OF YOUR AGE

key issue: *My New Life With God Can Start Where I Am Right Now*

Chapter 5   **page 69**

IN YOUR ILLNESS (DIS-EASE) YOU CAN GET IN A PLACE THROUGH YOUR SPIRIT TO GET HEALING

key issue: *Responding To God Through My Spirit Puts Me In A Better Position To Be Healed In My Total Being*

Chapter 6   **page 93**

YOU ARE A SPIRITUAL BEING AND THE SAVING OF YOUR SOUL IS YOUR WHOLE LIFE RESPOND-ING TO GOD

key issue: *My Whole Life Can Respond To God ... It Starts In My Spirit*

Chapter 7   page 97

HOW PRAYING WITH YOUR SPIRIT AND YOUR UNDERSTANDING WILL BRING YOU INTO CONSTANT BETTER HEALTH

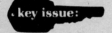 **key issue:**

My New Relationship With God Has A Language All Its Own

A SUMMARY OF STEP NUMBER ONE... 108

Step Number

TWO

**Your life will be completely
different *if* you learn to plant
good seed with God and
with people you like or dislike.**

Chapter 1 page 113

WHEN YOU DON'T LIKE GOD YOU ARE REALLY SAYING YOU DON'T LIKE ALWAYS TO RECOGNIZE GOD AS YOUR SOURCE

key issue:

I Will Look To God Alone As My Source And Not To People

Chapter 2 page 125

YOU MAY THINK YOU DISLIKE GOD WHEN THE TRUTH IS YOU JUST CAN'T STAND PEOPLE

key issue:

I Will Pray For People I Like Or Dislike Because God Loves Them All

Chapter 3 page 133

HOW A WHOLE CHURCH SOLVED ITS INSIDE PROBLEM OF BITTER- NESS

key issue:

Praying For Someone Else Will Begin A Healing In Me

Chapter 4   page 139

HOW A PERSONAL FRIEND LOST HIS WAY AND FOUND IT AGAIN— AND IF YOU FEEL A LITTLE LOST YOU CAN FIND YOUR WAY, TOO

key issue: *I Can Live My Life Right Every Day Through God My Source And My Strength*

Chapter 5   page 147

YOU MAY PANIC WHEN YOU REALLY START PLANTING SEED BY REACHING OUT TO PEOPLE—BUT EVEN WHEN YOU PANIC YOU CAN EXPECT A MIRACLE

key issue: *Even When It Scares Me I Will Plant Good Seed By Reaching Out To Others*

Chapter 6 **page 157**

HOW I LEARNED TO PLANT GOOD SEED THROUGH OBEDIENCE TO GOD WHEN HE TOLD ME TO TAKE HIS HEALING POWER TO THE PEOPLE

Reaching Out To Others Is Miracle Seed I Am Planting For My Own Healing And Success

A SUMMARY OF STEP NUMBER TWO...166

Step Number

THREE

You can expect many miracles for yourself if you have a right relationship with yourself . . . and with God.

Chapter 1   page 171

HOW TO LOVE YOURSELF AS GOD LOVES YOU SO YOU CAN LIVE IN A STATE OF BETTER HEALTH AND SUCCESS

• key issue:

I Am Using My Inborn Ability To Believe And Exercising My Faith To Get Well And Stay Well

Chapter 2   page 177

HOW TO AVOID WRONG BELIEVING THAT KEEPS YOU FROM BETTER HEALTH AND SUCCESS

• key issue:

I Value Every Instrument Of Healing, And Love The Source Of It All — God

Chapter 3   page 191

WHETHER YOU FEEL GOOD ENOUGH OR NOT YOU CAN STILL HAVE BETTER HEALTH AND SUCCESS

• key issue:

I Know Jesus Recognizes My Humanity And Wants To Heal Me Because I Am An Important Person

Chapter 4 page 203

HOW YOU CAN FREE YOURSELF FROM THE MYTH THAT EVERY BAD THING HAPPENING TO YOU IS GOD'S PUNISH-MENT

key issue: *All Sickness Is From The Devil...All Healing Is From God—I Am Believing God For His Best*

Chapter 5 page 219

HOW YOU CAN KNOW GOD LOVES YOU SO MUCH THAT HE WILL HEAL YOU EVEN THOUGH YOU HAVEN'T BELIEVED HE WOULD

key issue: *I Will Not "Fake It" About Any Illness—I Will "Faith It" Through To Healing*

21

Chapter 6   page 227

WHILE YOU ARE IN YOUR HUMAN SKIN YOU CAN STILL BREAK THROUGH TO GOD'S DIVINE HEALING POWER

key issue: *I Have A "Faith Miracle" In Me Every Second And I Will Accept It*

Chapter 7   page 233

HOW TO SUCCESSFULLY DEAL WITH YOUR DEADLY NEGATIVE EMOTIONS

key issue: *I Am Looking For New Dimensions For My Faith And Love To Shine Through To Others*

Chapter 8   page 251

HOW TO UNDERSTAND WHEN YOU NEED A PHYSICIAN AND SUGGESTIONS ON HOW AND WHEN TO GO TO A DOCTOR

key issue: *God Uses Prayer And Physicians To Complete His Healing Love In Me*

Chapter 9   page 261

WHEN THE DOCTORS SAY THERE IS NO HOPE AND PRAYER HAS APPARENTLY FAILED—HOW TO FACE THE FUTURE

 key issue:

I Face The Future Knowing My Life Is In God's Good Hands

Chapter 10   page 285

THE DAY WHEN YOU WILL BE TOTALLY HEALED

 key issue:

The Resurrection Is God's Perfect And Ultimate Healing

A SUMMARY OF STEP NUMBER THREE... 297

INTRODUCTION
by
James E. Winslow, Jr., M.D.
Dean of the School of Medicine
Oral Roberts University

When Oral Roberts told me he was writing another book, I asked him why. He said to me, "God has put it in my heart and I always try to obey God." Then when he began to tell me that the book was to deal with health, I asked him if I could write the introduction.

In my career as a medical doctor, I've never read anything more articulate in purpose or in content than *3 Most Important Steps To Your Better Health And Miracle Living*. It approaches the real problems of people who are sick and shows them how, where, and when to get help.

1. If you have a need—physical, spiritual, mental, financial, or a loved one in need—read this book. I can't think of anyone I know who won't be helped immeasurably by this book.

2. Every doctor should read this book. I believe that if I could have known what *3 Most Important Steps To Your Better Health And Miracle Living* is saying, I could have begun the practice of medicine with much more understanding of people that have physical needs. I could have become a more complete person and seen people as complete persons in terms of their needs and meeting those needs. In short, I believe it would have resulted in my being a better physician. Just as important, this book tells the reader how to be a patient. I wish all the patients I've had through the years had had the chance to read it.

3. If you are a minister, read *3 Most Important Steps To Your Better Health And Miracle Living.* Your ministry and work with the needs of people will never be the same.

4. If you face any problem at all in your relationship with God, with others, or even with yourself, read *3 Most Important Steps To Your Better Health and Miracle Living.*

I have been privileged to work with Oral Roberts for five years now. I first became involved with the University through my love for athletics by providing for the medical needs of the ORU athletic program. Then I treated Oral Roberts as a patient. In some of those rare times of relaxation he gets, we play golf and he has undertaken to cure my golf game—one of his very few failures in life, but there is still hope.

I agreed to serve on the Board of Regents at Oral Roberts University, first listening with awe and wonderment to his dreams, and then realizing that he meant every word he said about obeying God and building a major university on the Holy Spirit and under God's authority, with graduate schools including medicine. It was incredible, nearly impossible. I've learned by now, you see, to say *nearly* impossible, because saying impossible to Oral is like saying sic 'um to a wiry bulldog.

Finally, I agreed to conduct a study to determine what would be necessary for ORU to start its own Medical School. For more than a year, nearly every Saturday morning, he and I and others sat around his breakfast table discussing the Medical School project. One morning when the planning process seemed to be bogged down, I said, "Oral, are you sure God really wants you to build a medical school?"

He replied, "Yes." At last we called Evelyn into the room. She can get Oral to the key issue quicker and with less effort than anyone. She said, "Oral Roberts, are you positive that God told you to build this Medical School?"

At that Oral stood up and without a trace of doubt in his voice simply said, "God told me to do it. I can obey or disobey. I've been disobedient a time or two in the past and I will not knowingly disobey God again. I must build it. I hope you all will help me, but I must do it whether you do or not."

From that point on it became only a matter of how, not if, not why. Later, when he asked me to become the formative dean of the Medical School, I must confess I struggled with myself, with Oral, and with God before I finally agreed. But I had learned the secret to God's success through Oral Roberts—obedience to God's perfect will. God does not usually tell us what His will is for our lives and then allow us to sit down and choose either to do it or not to do it. We must be willing to obey God even before we know what His will is. That's what I see in Oral Roberts the person—a continual striving day by day to obey God.

What does this book offer you? *3 Most Important Steps To Your Better Health And Miracle Living* tells you in a practical, usable, everyday form, the theme of Oral Roberts' ministry. God wants you to be whole, i.e., well. Anything which removes you from a state of harmony with God, your fellowman, or normal human function, may be defined as an illness.

For 30 years Oral has been going about the world praying for people without regard to the nature of their sickness. I've never known a person so possessed with the urgency to see people healed and to live in health. He believes God is concerned for all your needs and he is excited about it. He believes God wants you to have spiritual health, to have emotional health, to have physical health, to be financially sound, to have good human relationships, to have a good job, to be able to earn your way. He is determined to obey God's command to carry all of God's healing power to his generation. God doesn't say some of His healing power or just part of it.

Since all healing originates with God, just as does every good and perfect gift, God intends for *all* His healing power to go to *all* His people. As children of God, we are entitled to that healing.

God utilizes many methods or delivery systems to bring His healing power to bear on our ailments. No one can measure or even comprehend the power of prayer. Yet prayer does not heal, neither does the one who prays; but God alone heals. Prayer puts the person who needs healing in position to be healed. It creates the proper condition required for the operation of God's healing power. We who work with Oral Roberts see this in his ministry and as he prays for the healing of people. God also uses physicians, dentists, and nurses to deliver His healing power. Yet neither they, their surgery, their medicine, nor their other treatments can heal. They can only create the best possible conditions in which God's healing power can function. Likewise, expressions of concern which one person shows for another person promote healing.

I am continually amazed that I still hear people who are sick ask themselves out loud, "Shall we pray for my healing or shall I go to the doctor?" Why shouldn't they do both? God wants to provide us with all His healing power, not just part of it. We have no right to limit God to one system or to another, particularly since He wants to heal us.

The chapters in this book demonstrate in very real terms how God brings His healing to people through different instruments. To the one desperate for healing, the instrument becomes less important than does the healing. In these pages, this generation's best authority on healing for the whole person tells you how to get into position for your healing. I hope as you read it you will be helped to direct your spirit, mind, and body toward total healing for you and your family. This is, I believe, what Oral Roberts wants more than anything in the world, and I do too.

AUTHOR'S NOTE:

Remember, be sure to read my Personal Word before you begin reading this book. My Personal Word will introduce you to how and why I wrote it.

Step Number

ONE

You will be in great position
to have health and success
if your relationship with
God your Source is right.

Chapter 1

HOW YOU CAN RECEIVE THE GREATEST MIRACLE YOU CAN EVER HAVE

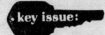 **key issue:** **I Will Put First Things First**

I think just about everybody has come across the terms, "getting saved," "receiving forgiveness of sins," "being born again," "having personal salvation."

If you haven't you will, or at least their equivalent.

I've gone through this myself. I've gone through it with thousands of others, and still do.

Speaking very frankly, getting your soul saved and continuing that kind of life through your lifespan will lead you to what I have so often said is the greatest miracle you will ever experience.

I mean the saving of your soul is the saving of you. It is your own personal salvation given to you from God. You are very important and Jesus says, "Ye must be born again" (John 3:7).

No *if* or *hope-so* or *maybe-so*—you must!

Better health and miracle-living are not accidents, although some people may appear to have health when their life-style is against God. But better health and miracle-living is much more than the physical health some have. I'm talking about total well-being—in the now . . . in the forever.

FIRST THINGS FIRST

Jesus said, "It is better for thee to enter halt into life, than having two feet to be cast into hell, into the fire that never shall be quenched" (Mark 9:45).

By that, Jesus doesn't mean that the members of your body, or your mind, are not important, but He seeks to help you put your priorities straight. First things first.

He tells you that your spirit is the most important part of you, and the healing and restoration of the spirit—from the disease of sin—is your most important healing.

MY PARENTS AND ME

My parents had a sense of sin and they tried to transmit this to me. They had a hard time convincing me that sin was the name of some things I was doing, that *I was a sinner.*

Me, a sinner?

How could I, a teen-ager, be a sinner? What had I done?

They kept saying, "Son, you must understand life from God's viewpoint, not your own."

They would read the Bible and have me listen. One verse made such an impression I can still quote it from memory:

"But your iniquities have separated between you and your God, and your sins have hid his face from you, that he will not hear" (Isaiah 59:2).

Another was a story Jesus told about two men—one self-righteous, telling how good he was and that there was nothing in his life that needed changing; the other recognized his life was not so good. This man bowed his head and said simply, "God, be merciful to me a sinner" (Luke 18:13). Jesus said it was this man who received God's approval and salvation, not the other man. That, too, impressed me.

As a teen-age rebel, even after I was long gone from parents, church, and God (or so I thought), I remembered these things from the Bible. I was able, however, to put them from my mind. My sins separated me from God. Consequently, God's face was hidden from me. And He wouldn't hear me so long as I persisted in ignoring Him. I was a sinner but these things didn't make the impact my parents had hoped.

There was something that happened to me that in hindsight I can see was a direct result of my parents' concern for my soul, and it's this: A sort of brooding feeling would arise in me from time to time, as if I knew there was something important I should act on and wouldn't, and had no intention of doing.

I became aware of God but didn't desire Him. What my parents had said, which was based on the Bible, was true. If I did change inwardly and let God direct my life it would be wonderful to them, but that didn't fit my personal plans and dreams.

I TURNED GOD OFF

A false picture of a life saved from sin presented itself to my mind. The strong dream of becoming a lawyer and, ultimately, governor of Oklahoma seemed totally unattainable if I were to become a saved person, so I turned off all feelings for God. However, He didn't turn His off for me. I still felt that haunting feeling inside that I should admit I was a sinner; I should ask for God's forgiveness and for personal salvation. But I didn't ask because I didn't want to. I didn't feel the need to.

I remember one day it was like God and I were in a room all alone. In my imagination I was facing Him. I felt crowded, uncomfortable, resentful, cheated that what I was dreaming might never, never happen. Crushed in my spirit over it, I fairly shouted, *"God, get out of my life. Let me alone."*

GOD LET ME ALONE

I thought that ended it since I felt a sort of release. As time wore on I slowly became aware of a happening inside me. *God had gotten out of my life. He had let me alone.*

At first, I thought, great! Then it wasn't so good. It was an eerie kind of feeling.

God had let me be on my own, to go it alone. Now I wasn't so sure I wanted it like this.

As a 17-year-old it hadn't occurred to me that people died, except very old people. My grandfather Roberts had died at 84, but that was an age many times my own and it seemed like an eternity.

But young people do die, even children. There doesn't seem to be any guarantee that anyone won't die at any age—young, middle-age, or old. People die.

Well, soon afterward I became very ill and in weeks was facing what seemed a sure early death.

Now you can think or say what you want, but I can assure you life can get very real, very quickly . . .

When I lay so many days upon the bed, unable to rise and getting worse instead of better, my parents were full of anguish and concern.

Papa would urge me to repent and get saved so I could go to heaven. I didn't know what it meant to repent, to get saved, and I certainly didn't want to go to heaven, anyway not then.

The fact was that Papa knew I was facing certain death and he wanted his baby boy to be in condition for his soul to go to heaven when his body died. He wanted the circle to be unbroken in heaven for his family.

Mamma would say, "Oral, pray, pray."

"I don't know how to pray, Mamma," I would reply.

This went on until one morning she said in a bright tone of voice, "Oh, son, you don't have to know how to pray. Just open your heart and talk to God as you would to me or to Papa. Tell Him you are sorry, then believe He hears you. God will do the rest."

Although I didn't respond that day, I heard what she said, "Son, you don't have to know how to pray—just talk to God . . ."

That hit home and made a lot of sense.

Now before we go any further I want you to do TWO things:

1. Read this Scripture:
"But your iniquities have separated between you and your God, and your sins have hid his face from you, that he will not hear" *(Isaiah 59:2).*

2. Then say the Key Issue: "I WILL PUT FIRST THINGS FIRST by beginning to

read and study the Scripture so that I can learn how to receive the greatest miracle of my life."

 I Will Put First Things First

Now, let's go to the next page.

Chapter 2

HOW YOU CAN BECOME AWARE OF SIN IN YOUR LIFE

 key issue: **I Am Aware Of My Need For A New Life**

Two things happened that brought me to a decision. These two things may seem unique to me but they really aren't, as you will see.

At that time I had made no connection with being saved from sin and being healed of tuberculosis and my stammering. I don't think my parents had. There was at that time (in the thinking of many people) quite a separation spiritually between the saving of the soul, and a cure coming to one's physical body. You prayed to God for your soul, and you went to the doctor for your body. Better health and miracle-living didn't seem to go with salvation. The possibility of miracles was pooh-poohed and little or none of it was taught either by religion or medicine.

In a way, it didn't seem a good time to get saved, nor a good time to turn oneself over to doctors. The distance and misunderstanding between them were too great, and I was caught in the middle. Still, both were legitimate—they needed only to get a little closer together, especially for persons like me who urgently needed both.

I WASN'T GOING TO MAKE IT

The first thing that I saw was I wasn't going to make it. If what my parents told me about my need of God and God's willingness to save me were true, then I should get serious about it.

The sense of sin though had not hit me, and I discovered that without it I couldn't concede I was a sinner.

This was taken care of in an unexpected way. While my parents gathered near my bed in family prayer, with the burden of their prayer for me, I looked up into Papa's face and what appeared to me in his countenance turned me around.

I thought I saw Jesus Christ in my father's face. The seeming image of Christ shone and my mind, through my eyes, saw it. I burst into tears. That apparent vision of the Man of Galilee was so real to my senses that involuntarily I called out, "O God, come into my life; save my soul." The sense of sin was on me unexplainably but clear. Moments later the presence of God came over me. I felt that God accepted me; I felt new and renewed inside.

HOW TO OPEN YOURSELF TO CHRIST

Having a need, and seeing something of Christ in another person that gives one a personal sense of his sins, are the two things I believe must happen *before anyone is willing* to think seriously about getting saved, or receiving what we know is salvation.

I don't mean a need necessarily like mine, which happened to be a direct need of physical healing. Nor do I mean one has to have some kind of spiritual vision of

Christ, as I did. But everybody has a need and everybody, I am convinced, will have some experience of God in the Person of Christ that is real to them. The *way* it happens is not as important as that it *does* happen. In other words, when you open your mind to Christ He will make himself known to you. You can depend on it happening—to you.

THE OLD SHEPHERD SAW THE GLORY

It's like the summer day a great scientist went up into the Scottish mountains to study a particular flower that was blooming at that time in all its glory. He wanted to look at it through his microscope without picking it in order to see it in all its perfection. He knelt down, adjusted his microscope, and soon was reveling in the flower's delicate color and beauty.

He was still in this position a few minutes later when a shadow fell across him. Looking up, he saw an old Highland shepherd watching him. Without saying a word, the scientist picked the flower and handed it, with the microscope, to the shepherd so that he too could see the beautiful sight. As the old shepherd looked, tears began streaming down his face. Then, handing the flower back very tenderly, he said, "Man, I wish you'd never shown me that."

"Why?" asked the scientist, puzzled.

"Because," he said, "these rude feet of mine have trodden on them so many times."

Something like this has got to happen to you concerning Christ and His glory for your life; and it will, I can assure you. That's when you, like me, want to get a new heart.

THE FIRST HEART TRANSPLANT

The first time I was on the Johnny Carson television show I followed a special guest, the famous heart transplant surgeon, Dr. Christian Barnard of South Africa. In the interview, Johnny asked Dr. Barnard what had been his most exciting experience in relation to his work.

Dr. Barnard said, "I believe the greatest experience of all happened one day as I was making a postoperative checkup on one of my patients. He said, 'Doctor, I wonder if you would let me see my old heart. I think it would help my attitude.' It was an unusual request, but I consented. Soon attendants wheeled in a big cart on which was a glass jar containing the man's heart."

Dr. Barnard said, "I took my pen and pointed to the problem area of his old heart. 'This,' I told him, 'is what would have killed you if you hadn't received a new heart.' The patient looked up and said with such gratitude, 'Doc, I'm so grateful you took out that old heart that was killing me and gave me a new heart!' "

That line expresses so aptly the joy of all those who receive a new heart—a spiritual transformation—from the Great Physician, Jesus Christ!

My new spiritual heart meant my spirit was reborn. The term, "responding first through your spirit," had not come to me then but that's exactly what I did. From deep within I felt hope that I would live and not die with the disease that was destroying me. Remarkable events began happening to me: my sister Jewel coming and saying, "Oral, God is going to heal you"—seven magic words, to me. My brother Elmer coming to pick me up and carry me for healing prayers. My being touched by

Christ's healing hands for a new beginning of life.

The gospel of Jesus Christ my parents had so faithfully tried to give me finally paid off—BIG.

PERSONAL SALVATION IS A POWERFUL STIMULANT TOWARD BETTER HEALTH

It is a very interesting fact that medical science has begun to take steps in this direction; at least it's talked about openly that the preaching of the gospel can produce a wholesome change in a person's life.

I recently read a book by Dr. Karl Menninger, the famous psychiatrist from Topeka, Kansas. In this book, *Whatever Became of Sin?* Dr. Menninger said, in effect, that we have lost our sense of sin, that the gospel is no longer being preached to the extent that people are aware of sin. *He says without this sense of sin there can be no full healing of the human personality.* Because when a person is engaged in wrong—such as being filled with bitterness, having hate in his heart, or striking at God—and he feels no awareness that he is doing wrong, it is a deadly deterrent to health.

THE HEALING PROCESS

Dr. Menninger says that *for peace of mind we must recapture the sense of sin.* Men must repent and receive God's forgiveness for their sins. Jesus has been saying that for a long time—*that in the healing process there must be forgiveness.* If there is something wrong inside we've got to get it out.

The hardest part is to become aware that you need saving, to admit you are a sinner, and that you are saved by a Person, only by a Person and only by the Person of Jesus Christ. This begins with feeling a sense of sin.

HOW TO DEAL WITH SIN IN YOUR LIFE

You will hear me say again and again, God's greatest miracle is being saved.

We hear people say:

"The operation saved me."

"I was in an accident but I was saved."

"I came out of it and now everything is going to be all right."

They mean, of course, coming through some bad incident.

What I mean about being saved is more than that, much more.

I mean the saving of your S-O-U-L. Your inner self made in the image and likeness of God. Your spirit which is what you are and which needs a new birth. Really your total self being saved.

So you can become aware of a sense of sin in your life, I want you to repeat these four specific things. Say them out loud.

1. *I am aware of my need for a new life.*

2. I will pray that I will see Christ re-flected in another person's life.

3. To be aware of a sense of sin and do something about it can bring full healing of my whole person.

4. In my healing process, I will begin practicing forgiveness because this opens me up to my healing.

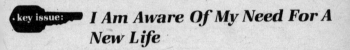 **key issue:** *I Am Aware Of My Need For A New Life*

Now, let's go on.

Chapter 3

IT'S NOT YOUR FAULT YOU ARE A SINNER, BUT IT IS IF YOU DON'T DO SOMETHING ABOUT IT

 key issue: I Am On The Road To A New Life And Better Health Because Of God My Source

I'm often asked, "But how do I know I am a sinner?"

Think of being a sin-ner. When you disobey God, you have sinned. Disobeying and being sorry for it so that you ask forgiveness and begin anew with determination to joyously obey God is one thing; to disobey and keep on disobeying—that is not only sin, it makes you a sinner or sin-ner.

The Bible teaches that you are born with this ability and desire to sin. Through your power of choice you very early began a series of rebellions against God. Fortunately, some recognize this as an experience of youth and as an adolescent, change; others harden in it and become a sin-ner.

A sin-ner reaches the point in his choice of the kind of life he will live, that he is going to live *his* way, do *his* thing, without calling on God and without looking to God as his Source. He goes a step further by deciding he is going to do this in his life and carry it with him into death. From God's viewpoint, he has "hardened his heart."

A SIN-NER HAS TWO CHOICES

One, he can realize the Bible's way to salvation, "Now is the day of salvation" (2 Corinthians 6:2), so "harden not your hearts" (Hebrews 3:8).

Two, he can continue keeping his spirit down by living only in his intellect and physical senses, which is in direct disobedience and opposition to the way God created man.

If he takes the first choice, as I did (and do every day), he will recognize his acts of disobedience as sin, and will eventually come to the point of "changing his mind," which is what repentance is. He will change his mind about trying to run his life with his intellect and physical senses and return to his spirit, or to himself as a spiritual being. Like the prodigal son Jesus refers to in Luke 15, who "when he came to himself, and said...I will arise and go to my father, and will say unto him...Father, I have sinned against heaven, and in thy sight," he will do the same thing and find the Father lovingly waiting to receive him and restore his spirit to its proper place of governing his life. This places his mind and body in their proper place and creates the new man in Christ Jesus—the whole man, or the full human being again.

If he chooses the second step which is to continue in sin until his heart is hardened, making him a sin-ner, then He will have NO SOURCE for his life on earth. He will be like the man whose marriage was in trouble, also his morals, and in asking for my help, heard me tell him about Jesus being able to work out his problems, said, "But, Oral, what does this guy Jesus have to do with it anyway?"

"Jesus has everything to do with it!" I replied.

"Why?" he asked.

"Because He is your Savior AND YOUR SOURCE. Without Him in your life, and without your looking to Him as the Source of your total supply, you have cut yourself off from God like a limb is cut off from the tree."

"Oh," he said, "I'm glad you explained it that way. I hadn't thought of it that way before."

Not only do you have no Source but at death you will have carried being a sin-ner into death *and the judgment.* Remember, God said, "It is appointed unto men once to die, and after this the judgment" (Hebrews 9:27).

A STORY OF TWO BROTHERS

I read about two brothers some time ago. One of them was a fair, just, and hard-working man. The other brother was a ne'er-do-well who was always getting into trouble. However, he knew he could always depend on the stable brother to get him out of his troubles. He'd helped him so many times that one day the wayward brother decided that no matter what he did his good brother could get him out.

Years passed and the wayward brother continued to sin, paying little attention to his brother's life and the things he was accomplishing. Among these accomplishments was that he had become a judge.

Finally the wayward brother was apprehended again and brought into court. As he sat down he looked up and there was the judge coming to the bench in his judicial robes. He recognized that the judge was his own brother who had always gotten him out of trouble. Quickly he began to signal with his hands. Fantically he motioned to the judge—"Remember me, I'm your brother. I'm your brother! Look over here and get me out—I'm your brother!"

But the brother who had become a judge looked at him as he would any other man brought into court. Eventually the trial was over and the judge pronounced sentence on his own brother. It was the first time the court had seen the judge shed tears. As the authorities took the condemned man away he shouted, "But I am your brother—and you are *my* brother—you always got me out of trouble before."

The judge, with tears streaming down his cheeks, said, "Yes. Yesterday I was your brother but today I am your judge." And that's exactly the way it is with you and Christ. Today He is here to save you. But if you continue going in your own ways, rejecting the repeated mercies of Christ to you, then one day you will face Him in the position that He must assume—your eternal judge in justice according to your sins.

YOU ARE IMPORTANT

Let me tell you, neither you nor I deal with something casual and unimportant when we deal with our lives. The Bible says, "God is not a man, that he should lie" (Numbers 23:19).

God doesn't lie. The Bible is His revealed Word. It is the truth about God, about man, about life, about death, and the judgment. I value it above all books. As I said about the library at Oral Roberts University when we opened in 1965, "The ORU library has tens of thousands of books, new and old, and will have many more over the years. These books will contain much of the known knowledge of man. But there is one Book that is greater than all the books of this library, or of the whole world. It's the Holy Bible. It's our key book, central to our existence and operation as a university, and central to the success of our personal lives."

I added, "If we were able to teach our students all the knowledge contained in all the books and periodicals in our library, it would never be enough. This knowledge might stimulate their intellect but only the Bible can fully nourish their spiritual beings. If we can begin in our spirit with the Bible, and work from it into these great publications of man's knowledge, we will fulfill our reason for being a university — to *educate the whole man*."

I believed that in 1965 in our beginning. I believe it more today as we have added our medical, dental, law, business, and other colleges to the Oral Roberts University.

The two greatest things about the Bible for you in a practical way is that it gives you the Man Christ Jesus who is...

> the Way,
> > the Truth,
> > > and
> > > > the Life
> > > > > (John 14:6).

And it gives you Seed-Faith, making your life a seed you plant, which is the giving of yourself in love and concern as Jesus does. Seed-Faith enables you to: (1) love God by making Him your Lord and your Source; (2) love your neighbor as you love yourself; Seed-Faith produces miracle harvests back in the form of your needs so that what St. Paul says literally happens, "But my God shall supply all your need according to his riches in glory by Christ Jesus" (Philippians 4:19); (3) expect a miracle from your seed sown, knowing God your Source has a "due season" for you to reap your miracle harvest (Galatians 6:9). I cannot overemphasize the value to your health in Seed-Faith living. In a powerful, positive way it touches every part of your life — every day.

STEPS IN BEING BORN AGAIN

I know as you read this book you will want a new life. You want to be born again and to know it. You want to know the steps to take.

First, come to the point in your life that you recognize you are committing sins and are a sinner, for "all have sinned, and come short of the glory of God" (Romans 3:23). This will lead you to the Savior; if you don't recognize you are a sinner, it will lead you into becoming a sin-ner, meaning you will carry your sins into death and into the judgment. You will have made up your mind to be a sin-ner forever. If you do this, the Bible tells you that you will be forever lost; you will choose to go to hell. There will be no recourse, you will go to hell. And you will go there not by God's choice, since He gave His only begotten Son that you should be saved and not be lost. No. You will go there only if you choose to reject God and go there because you want to go there. It will be your own choice.

Now I'm not a hellfire and brimstone preacher. But I assure you I respect the fact of a hell. I am influenced by it and I don't intend to have hell in me while I live on earth, nor do I intend to go to hell after death.

So it's very important that you see yourself as you are, a sinner on the way to becoming irrevocably a sin-ner (one who continues to sin and who rejects salvation).

When I realized I was a sinner, that was my first step to God. It led me to the sinner's prayer which Jesus indicated is, *Lord, be merciful to me a sinner*, and in that moment I prayed those words and asked Christ to save me.

Second, tell God you want Him as your Savior, as your Source. You can only do this sincerely when you recognize that you need Him, that you know only *He* can save you and be the Source of your total supply.

Wanting God is a process of absorbing—it's finding you are absorbing Him as a person into your spirit and into your mind and body—into yourself as a Person.

Third, receive Christ, receive Him as a Person. You have been "getting" or trying to all your life. But *receiving* in this sense is different from getting or being a getter. It's a little more difficult, in a way, to receive. Saying "I'll get this guy" or, "I'll get this thing" or, "I'll get this deal," is not the same as, "I'll receive Christ into my heart as my personal Savior and Source."

In receiving, you have first given. What do you give? You give your sins to God, you give Him your past mistakes, you give Him all your past. You give Him today. Then you determine you will give Him your entire future. Forever and ever you are giving yourself to God. That is, you'll be striving to give yourself daily to Him. Your start is a onetime thing but your continuing is more; it is a continuous series of loving by giving yourself. You'll find new ways to love or give of yourself. This is true Seed-Faith living.

It's in this spirit of giving to Him that your seed of faith is planted, and from this planting you will RECEIVE. You receive the Living Christ, the greatest miracle of all. He comes in and you receive Him not as a guest but as your Savior and Lord...and as your Source. In a very real sense it is important to you to *daily* receive Christ.

The most helpful thing to me in having given myself and my sins to God is that I meant it. The start I made at 17 was a real decision I made. It was something I felt to the core of my being. It was no flash-in-the-pan kind of thing. The sin-ner had been changed to a Christian. Christian, I am told, means "little Christ." We are remade in His image and likeness. Christian means we will carry Him in us through life, and into death and the resurrection and life with Him forever.

Fourth, recognize in the process of Christ's giving you a new birth, taking you into Him and bringing himself into you, of saving your soul—in all this, *it is the work of the Holy Spirit who brings Christ into your being.*

Who is the Holy Spirit? The Holy Spirit is the other "Comforter" (John 14:16). He is the One whom Christ said He would send back to replace His own physical presence on earth. The Holy Spirit is Christ coming back in His own invisible, unlimited form to (live) "in" you and to abide "with" you forever (John 14:16,17).

You see, God is one God. "O Israel: The Lord our God is one Lord" (Deuteronomy 6:4). When we call Him Father, Son, and Holy Spirit—the Holy Trinity—we are not saying He is three Gods. He is simply God...God manifesting himself as the *Father* with a specific work to do, as the *Son* with a specific work to do, and as the *Holy Spirit* with a specific work to do.

As an example, let's take water. It can manifest itself in three ways: as liquid, as ice, or as vapor. But it is still water.

SON OF GOD

The same is true of God. As God loving us, He came to earth as *the Son* to be born of a woman, to become a human being and (1) to show us what He (God) is like: loving and good, (2) to sit where we sit, feel what we feel, go through all we experience, and show us the way through it, and (3) to give himself as the divine seed on the cross for our sins, that seed becoming the miracle harvest of the resurrection so that we, too, will rise from the dead and live forever.

HOLY SPIRIT

After Christ divested himself of His human body by being raised from the dead and ascending back to heaven, He prayed the Father to send the Holy Spirit. So the Father manifested himself as the Holy Spirit —not as the Son in the flesh but Spirit which He is—who comes into our spirit.

Remember, God originally made man a spirit. He didn't make him mind or body only. He made him a living soul and gave him a mind and body.

So Holy Spirit is God himself, but without the limitations of the human body of Jesus which was limited to time, to space, and to death, as each of us is.

To be without these limitations He is now invisible (and in us) where they can never crucify Him again. He is also unlimited so that time, space, or death can never touch Him again. Therefore, the Holy Spirit in you is invisible; He is unlimited. This puts you into miracle living. It makes all things possible to you (Matthew 17:20). Through the indwelling Holy Spirit, who is Christ returned in His invisible, unlimited form in you, you are in position to enter into miracle-living. You have God's original basis on which to have better health for your total being.

This is why seeking health is misleading. You don't seek health, which is a thing, you seek God who is the Source of your health. You don't go to a doctor expecting him to be the source of giving you health. God is your Source and the doctor is one of the instruments He uses for health, and medicine is one of God's delivery systems for your health care. But the Source of both, the skill of the doctor and the healing properties of the medicine IS GOD!

Once you get this point clear in your mind—that you start with God your Source and then seek the help of His instruments such as prayer, or medicine, or a combination of both, then you are on the right road to better health in every aspect of your life.

The same is true in regard to the church. You don't attend the church service as an end in itself; it too is an extension of the Living Christ through the Holy Spirit —it's like taking your car to a service station, not to park it but to have it serviced to carry you where you need to go.

Nothing is a Source but G-O-D. Say it, "God is my Source."

Here is what you can do if you no longer want to be a sinner:

1. Recognize you are a sinner—say it: "I AM A SINNER. For all have sinned and come short of the glory of God" (Romans 3:23).

2. Tell God you want Him as your Savior and Source for your life. Say it: "God, I want You as the Savior and Source for my life."

3. Receive Christ as a Person by giving Him your sins. Then give Him your future—ALL of it. Say it: "I give You my sins—I give You my future, ALL of it."

4. Recognize that receiving Christ is the work of the Holy Spirit in your life (John 15:26). Say it: "I recognize the Holy Spirit as the One who brings Christ into my life."

 key issue: *I Am On The Road To A New Life And Better Health Because Of God My Source*

Chapter 4

HOW TO KNOW YOU ARE BORN AGAIN REGARDLESS OF YOUR AGE

● key issue: My New Life With God Can Start Where I Am Right Now

He was an old man now, nearly 84. I had read a book about him, how he had faced adversity of almost every kind to rise from a laborer at a sawmill to a giant in the furniture-making industry. He had many plants and thousands of employees who had great affection for the man who provided them with work and a generous profit-sharing plan. His sons were outstanding—one in public life, one heading the operations of the plants, the others doing well.

This man was known for his generous spirit and was well thought of by many.

We started getting letters from him two or three years ago in which he stated appreciation for our television ministry, and how his inner life was inspired by my sermons and prayers both on television and in my books.

One day I appeared in a certain area when, as I walked into the building, a man said, "You're Oral Roberts, aren't you?" I said, "Yes, I am." "Well, there's a man on the phone here asking for you," and he handed me the receiver.

The voice on the other end said, "Dr. Roberts?"

"Yes?"

"I am . . ." and he told me his name.

"Yes?"

"You remember I've been writing to you for your prayers."

"I remember a person by that name but I don't believe I have met you personally."

"You have not, and that is the object of my phone call. I feel elated I reached you like this since I had a hunch to call you at this phone, not knowing for sure if you would be there...but you are."

"What can I do for you?"

"You can pray for me."

"I've been doing that."

"Well, I'm only a short distance away and my son is standing by to drive me. Would you pray for me if I come?"

"Certainly," I said, "just be here in about a half hour and we'll find a quiet corner for the prayer."

When we met, I saw a man who looked like a man of strength and courage. For his years he appeared healthy. He said, "My back needs healing. The surgeons over the years have kept me going but they feel, and I feel, I'm going to need a special touch, a miracle as you call it. Would you help me?"

TOUCHING EACH OTHER

I pointed out that since I could not heal but was an instrument of our Lord's healing power, I wanted him to think particularly of Jesus' hands when we joined hands, and suggested we pray for one another.

"You mean you want me to pray for you?" he asked.

"Yes," I replied, "that's *planting a seed of faith*, that's giving of your concern and faith for someone else, as the Bible teaches in James 5:16, 'Pray one for another that ye may be healed,'—that is, the seed you plant in some one else's life will come back to you in the form of your need. Then I will pray for you as a seed I plant and God will bless us both."

He said, "I would like very much to do as you ask: pray for you, and I do pray but really I don't feel I can pray effectively. You see, I want to be sure I am born again."

I immediately sensed this was the *key issue*. This was why he had come. His back was troubling him and he knew I would be concerned for his healing. He knew deep within him that it was absolutely essential that he be born again by the Spirit of God and that he know it beyond any doubt.

At 84, not even the vast achievements he had accomplished would suffice. Being born again is absolutely essential to better health and miracle-living at 84 or any age. And I knew he could have both the new birth *and* help for his back and I told him so. "God is interested in whole-man healing. Everything about you is important to Him."

As I reached my hands to his for the dual prayer—or what I call the Seed-Faith prayer—I saw the strained look on his face.

"Is there something else wrong?" I asked.

"Well, I . . . I . . . just want to be sure that I am born again. I've been troubled about it a great many years. Your coming to this area brought it to the surface and I want it very much . . . I want the life our Lord promised . . . I want life . . ." and his voice trailed off.

THE SINNER'S PRAYER

Abruptly I said, "Please repeat after me the sinner's prayer which Jesus gave in the Bible:

> Lord,
> be merciful
> to me
> a sinner.

Slowly, with obvious deep feeling, he said, "Lord, be merciful to me . . . to me . . . a sinner."

"Now," I said, "tell God you believe He heard you and you believe He receives you as a newborn child in His kingdom."

He thanked the Lord and said, "Lord, I believe." When he looked at me again, I said, "If you meant this from your spirit first, letting it work on up through your mind and physical senses, you will be born again. You will feel it in the innermost depths of your being. Divine life will flow from within you and the Holy Spirit will fill your life."

He smiled. "Yes, I'm beginning to experience it now."

Then: "This is so important to me, I've been so long wanting God to let me know I am born again. Now it's here."

We rejoiced together. "What about your back?"

"Oh, yes," he replied. "You think He will help me there, too?"

"All of you is His. Your body is a temple of His Spirit and you are to glorify God with your body as you do with your spirit and mind—with your whole self."

Taking out my pocket-size New Testament I read to him from 1 Corinthians 6:19,20: "Know ye not that your body is the temple of the Holy Spirit which is in you, which you have of God, and ye are not your own? For ye are bought with a price: therefore glorify God in your body, and in your spirit, which are God's."

PRAYING AS A SEED YOU PLANT

I said, "God wants you—the total you—to be in better health. There's a miracle for your back just the same as for your soul's being born again. Now let's join hands again and as you pray for me, make it a seed for God to multiply back in healing for your back."

When the prayer was over he said, "This is some experience for me. I believe God has seen fit to answer my prayers. I've tried to be a good man, working hard and helping people. But this makes a great difference."

I said, "Yes, it means your last years can be your best years. Learn to live in Seed-Faith."

He smiled, "Reverend Roberts, I've been reading and studying your Seed-Faith book for months now, and your book, *A Daily Guide To Miracles And Successful Living Through Seed-Faith*, is of immeasurable help to me. I never miss one of your telecasts. I've made up my mind to fly to Tulsa and see your Prayer Tower."

"You are welcome," I said. "Many thousands visit the Prayer Tower at the Oral Roberts University each year. Many of them write me notes on how they felt God the moment they drove onto the campus."

On leaving he said, "Being born again is important, isn't it?"

I said, "So important that Jesus said in John 3:3-5 that it is the only way you can see and enter the kingdom of God. I was born again at age 17 and I feel it's just as important to me now as it was then—it means my life is in God and it means the same for you and everyone who wants abundant and eternal life."

I can see him now as he got into the car, looking at me and waving, and being driven away. What I see is his beaming face. It said, "I am born again."

IN THE BIG CRUSADES

From 1947 through 1968 I conducted evangelistic crusades before large audiences throughout America and all the continents. In every service, in every sermon, in every healing line I would always say, "God's greatest miracle is the saving of your soul."

Since 1968 when I felt God wanted me to concentrate most of my ministry on weekly television, plus quarterly prime-time Specials (and since TV is where the people are), I have continued saying, "God's greatest miracle is the saving of your soul." Sometimes I use other phrases meaning the same thing: being born again, or, God forgiving your sins, or, accepting Christ as your personal Savior. These are synonymous terms meaning you are made a new creature in Jesus Christ (2 Corinthians 5:17).

But I go a step further now. I talk about a whole man being saved—spirit, mind, and body. This is top priority for me, for you, for everyone. I call it whole-man healing, whole-man salvation. Or simply becoming a full human being again as God intended when He made man in His own image and likeness (Genesis 1:26). To better understand this, let me share with you . . .

THE FALL OF MAN

When man fell from the state of God's image and likeness it was a choice he made to live without God, to go it on his own, to put his spirit down and elevate his mind so that his response to life would be through his intellect (mind) and body (physical senses), rather than responding first in his spirit as God had intended.

His choice to live without God was an act of disobedience and it became sin to him, and sin separated him from God who had created him.

I want to emphasize that the consequences of his choice were produced by his choice. God had created and chosen him and given him many gifts:

1. The gift of His own moral and spiritual likeness, making him a spiritual being with a mind and body—and as such, a full human being.

2. The gift of dominion and power, to rule over everything on earth.

3. The gift of communication with God, to walk with his Creator, to talk with Him, to live in oneness and fellowship with Him. This was a priceless gift. Millions would give anything in the world if they only knew how to be able to talk directly and comfortably with God, and have Him respond in the same way.

4. The gift of the power of choice. To choose God or Satan. To choose to recognize himself as a spiritual being with a mind and body

making him a whole person, or to choose to
replace his spirit with his mind (or intellec-
tually pursuing life rather than responding
first through his spirit, which is the way God
made him). Man's power of choice lifted him
above all living things and creatures since he
alone can choose. The evil, the chaos, the
wars, the fears, the pain — all of it — is a result
of man's own choice which he used against
God and, as it has turned out, against
himself and other living things.

Because of his sin, and his choice to go his own
way, man was driven from the Garden of Eden, the
perfect habitat in which God placed him. There, he
had been given work which was to tend and dress
the garden. There, he was in fellowship with God
and with the woman God gave him. There, he was
a many-splendored creature in a many-splendored
environment.

The fateful decision was his and his alone. Staying
with God as He made him, man never would have
experienced sin or sickness or want or death.

SPIRIT IS STILL DOMINANT

God made him a spirit and placed the true
governing power of his life in his spirit. Although
man chose to put his spirit down by elevating his
mind and body over it; nevertheless, his spirit is still
the dominant part of his being. It is in a state of
death, meaning it is separated from God, his Source.
It is in this state of separation from the Creator that
man's spirit continues to wreak havoc upon his life.

Remember when God had made man's body from the dust of the ground, or the elements of the earth, He went beyond that and did something very, very special. He breathed His own life into the nostrils of man's body and man became a living soul or spirit. Jesus explained the reason for it in John 4:24, "God is a Spirit: and they that worship him must worship him in spirit and in truth."

Concerning man's spiritual death or his separation from God, the prophet Isaiah spoke of it like this, "But your iniquities have separated between you and your God, and your sins have hid his face from you, that he will not hear" (Isaiah 59:2).

Man had separated himself from God by deliberate choice. As a result he is described as having a "heart deceitful above all things, and desperately wicked" (Jeremiah 17:9).

You need to accept this so you know how you arrived at being a sinner. I am thrilled to tell you...

You can know you are born again regardless of your age by:

1. Repeating the sinner's prayer ... Do it: "God, be merciful to me a sinner" (Luke 18:13).

2. Praying for others now as a seed you plant. Here is a sample prayer: "Lord Jesus, thank You for healing ..."

(Write name of person.)

3. Now say, "I will start learning how to respond to God through my spirit."

My New Life With God Can Start Where I Am Right Now

Chapter 5

IN YOUR ILLNESS (DIS-EASE) YOU CAN GET IN A PLACE THROUGH YOUR SPIRIT TO GET HEALING

 key issue: **Responding To God Through My Spirit Puts Me In A Better Position To Be Healed In My Total Being**

The most exciting discovery that you can make is to know that you can move toward becoming a complete personality—whole in spirit, mind, and body. GOD CAN WORK WONDERS OF HEALING IN YOUR LIFE. I say this because in dealing with thousands of people through the years I have discovered that . . .

DIS-EASE IS DIS-HARMONY

I. WHAT HAS HAPPENED?

Disease (pronounced dis-ease) means *something out of order in the system.* God made the whole universe in perfect order. If anything were to get out of order in the universe, it would produce disharmony and a catastrophe. Your body is a miniature universe made by the hand of God. When everything is in order, every organ functions as it is intended to function.

Generally speaking, a system is defined as an assemblage of objects which are united by some form of regular interaction. Webster's Dictionary gives as specific examples of systems: "1. The universe. 2. The body considered as a functional unit." Therefore, *it is just as unnatural for the human body to come into a state of functional disorder as it would be for the universe to break down in its planned interactions.*

So sickness, or dis-ease, is maladjustment of a system. *As related to the human body,* this could be
the skeletal system,
the nervous system,
the respiratory system,
and other systemic functions
of your body.

As applied to your life, sickness can be
physical,
mental,
spiritual.

Whatever takes away from your peace of mind, your happiness, your normal comfort, your general well-being is dis-ease.

Anything that brings disharmony, discomfort, or distress physically, mentally, or spiritually is a form of illness. And from that standpoint, *I believe . . .*

EVERYBODY NEEDS HEALING

Oh, you may not need healing for your body. You may need healing for your emotions. It could be healing for your soul. It could be healing for your marriage, for your finances, for your relationships. It could be that your business needs a healing. It could be to find the power "just to get by from payday to payday," as one young couple suffering with money needs said to me, and who also asked me to pray for a healing for this in their lives. Or it could be a healing for your body or that of a loved one.

It is God's highest wish for us to prosper and be in health, even as our soul prospers, and that this prosperity be in ALL THINGS and in EVERY WAY. "Beloved, I wish above all things that thou mayest prosper and be in health, even as thy soul prospereth" (3 John 2).

For example, God gave me a miracle with my youngest son, Richard, who went away from me like I went away from my father when I was a teen-ager. Then one day a miracle happened . . .

It was a healing!

Richard wasn't ill physically but he received a healing from God in his spirit and in his emotions. And now instead of saying what he used to say so bitterly, "Dad, get off my back," he says with a real conviction, "Dad, you are no longer on my back. I am by your side." And he really is. He is the featured singer on the *Oral Roberts and You* television program and our prime-time quarterly specials. He is also at my side in a leadership capacity as we conduct the business affairs of the ministry. And even more recently, he and his dear wife, Patti, are conducting Partners' Meetings of their own all across the country, and with great results. I tell you, that's the sweetest news a father can ever hear from his son or daughter! You see, this healing started *inside*.

WHAT A SURGEON SAID TO ME ABOUT A MIRACLE HEALING IN THE BIBLE

The miracle healing of the man with the withered hand, recorded in Mark 3:1-5, says that the healing of your total self is what God has in mind. In this, God sees a cure or a healing differently than man does. For example, here was a man who had a limp, useless hand. But Jesus did not focus His attention solely on the man's hand. He first spoke to the man himself and said, "Stand forth." *You* is implied here, meaning, "You stand forth!"

An orthopedic surgeon, who is a friend of mine, was talking to me about this particular miracle. He said, "Oral, as a doctor I would have automatically turned my attention to the man's hand. This goes back to my medical training. But as I read this story I noticed that Christ did not touch the man's crippled hand. He seemed to view it as an extension of the man's entire personality . . . and within the healing of the whole man, his hand was restored."

Then my friend added a statement that I thought was tremendous. He said, "More and more I believe medicine is moving in this direction—toward whole man healing."

Isn't that exciting? Jesus is the restorer of the human being—the healer of your whole person—*body, mind, and spirit*—and medicine is moving in that direction!

WHOLE IS SOMETHING YOUR FAITH CAN "MAKE" YOU

Time and time again during the ministry of Jesus, He spoke the healing word like this: *Thy faith hath made thee whole.* The word *whole* means complete, well, sound, healthy—or well-being in your total self.

This should be your will too. You should commit yourself to being "made" a whole person. Better health and miracle-living is not only possible in your life—it is your God-given right!

And the only way to begin your journey to making you whole is to begin in your spirit—which God created in His spiritual and moral likeness. This likeness or image is God's essence, the essence of His own being. To be born of God in your spirit today is a restoration of God's own essence or nature to yourself. You take on this spiritual reality in your being. Through it you can learn to respond to every situation you face by using your spirit—your inner self—then let this response flow up through your mind and body until your response is the whole-person response. You can face dis-ease or dis-harmony as God made you to respond—from your spirit, which is God's own way of doing it.

Learning the way God made you (and remakes you by giving you a new spiritual rebirth) . . . learning the way God does things and trying by faith to do them as He does . . . learning that although you are flesh (human) you can respond to life first through the spiritual nature God re-creates in you . . . learning these all-important things about God, about yourself and your response to whatever you face in life; that, my friend, is the beginning of a whole new life in which you have a real opportunity to be made a whole human being.

This excites me and I hope it excites you and will keep you excited the rest of your life!

YOUR RESTORATION TO WHOLENESS IS GOD'S IDEA

There is no record of anyone's having begged God to redeem or restore mankind to wholeness. No human being thought of it. But *God thought of it*, planned, and executed it without being asked. "He (Jesus) shall bruise thy (the devil's) head" (Genesis 3:15).

The Old Testament ends with a threat . . . God calling upon the people to repent of their disobedience and to change, lest He come and smite the earth with a curse (Malachi 4:6). The New Testament begins with the birth of a Baby and the promise of life—abundant life.

In Matthew 1:21 we read:

> *Thou shalt call his name JESUS: for*
> *he shall save his people from their sins.*

In John 10:10 we read:

> *I am come that they might have life,*
> *and have it more abundantly.*

Jesus is not only a Savior from sin but also a Savior of *persons*. The word *saved* comes from the same root word for "heal." So this verse really means:

> "You shall call His name JESUS for He
> shall *heal* persons. He shall *heal*
> them from their sins, their shortcomings,
> their failures, the disharmony
> in their nature. He shall *heal* their
> bodies, their minds—*their whole beings.*
> He shall give them *abundant* life."

How does Jesus do this? He begins in the Spirit. You see, Jesus, the Man, had to be born and it was the Holy Spirit who conceived Him (Matthew 1:20). This is why Jesus said: *Ye must be born again. Except a man be born . . . of the Spirit, he cannot enter into the kingdom of God* (John 3:5-7).

Let's get back to basics. Jesus didn't say, "Ye must be born of the mind . . . or of the body." *Ye must be born of the spirit*! Jesus recaptured the possibility of a new birth so you can be reborn in the spiritual and moral likeness of God. No longer must you be separated from God. No longer must your spirit be put down. But once again your spirit will be put in charge and made the source of your total response to life. This is the new birth, or second birth, that Jesus says you must have following your own natural physical birth.

ALL YOUR PROBLEMS ARE SPIRITUALLY BASED

When Jesus came, He was concerned with the concerns of people. He healed all kinds of problems—sickness, poverty, marital trouble, soul needs, money needs, emotional needs. Each time, Christ approached the person not merely from the standpoint of his problem but from the standpoint of his whole person being restored. For, actually, because we are spiritual beings all our problems *are spiritually based*. Oh, we may feel a problem physically. We may feel it financially. We may feel it emotionally. But all *problems have a spiritual basis*.

> *And the Lord God formed man of the dust of the ground, and breathed*

*into his nostrils the breath of
life; and man became a living soul*
(Genesis 2:7).

Man became a *living* soul—a *spiritual* being!!

From the moment of creation God showed that man's *spirit*—not his mind or his body—is to be the governing power of his life on earth. Man's spirit is to have supremacy over the mind and body and bring them together into a unified, harmonized whole man in which God would live "in" the person. Also, that a person will live "in" God. "For in him we live, and move, and have our being; as certain also of your own poets have said, For we are also his offspring" (Acts 17:28).

We see God "in" man and man "in" God in the Garden of Eden when God and man walked and talked in a togetherness. Man's life and breath and being were coordinated in this original relationship with God. God's delight was evident in His closeness to man. God said, "It was very good" (Genesis 1:31). When something is good, it works; it's wonderful.

What was good to begin with was man's understanding that he was a spiritual being. As long as he chose to keep that in proper focus he would have great well-being and success. It would be miracle-living at its highest.

You see, YOUR WHOLE LIFE IS SPIRITUALLY BASED! The problems or needs you have may look physical, but that's just the way they appear to you. Your every problem begins in your spirit and the solution to it begins in your spirit.So to get an answer for your problems, you've got to get back into the *spirit —God's Spirit and your spirit*—the way you were made —and the way *God remakes you* when you repent of your sins and believe on Jesus as your personal Savior and then experience His Holy Spirit working in your life every day.

GOD'S MATERIAL

The tree of knowledge in the Garden of Eden was beautiful to look upon and good to the taste; *it appealed to the senses.* But because God had made Adam and Eve a spirit, and to respond to life from their spirit first, He had forbidden them to eat of the tree of knowledge or to live on the level of the physical and intellectual senses only. Therefore, when they ate of the forbidden fruit, the Bible says that immediately "they *knew*" (Genesis 3:6,7).

In that moment—as a result of that choice—man's spirit was submerged and he chose to live by his intellect. When the mind ascended above the spirit, taking over, the spiritual part of man died—*or ceased to function as the source of his response to God and to life.*

In that moment man chose to live only on the level of his senses—what appeals to his sight, hearing, feeling, taste, and smell—on the materialistic, sensual level of life.

From that moment man decided he was going to manage his life and do what he wanted to do. No longer would he exist as God had made him. He was saying, "God, I don't need You; with my intellect (mind) I can run my own life."

From that moment there was a disintegration of the personality of man—a separation or fragmentation of his spirit, mind, and body—and thus a lack of harmony and peace. This is why it is estimated that 85 percent of our diseases are emotionally induced. The mind alone cannot cope with the frictions of life, and it passes off to the body its limitations, frustrations, fears, and torments.

From that moment man was no longer God's masterpiece. But, thank God, we are still God's material! And through Jesus Christ, God's Son, we can be "made whole." St. Paul says in Romans 8:13, "For if ye live after the flesh, ye shall die: but if ye through the Spirit do mortify the deeds of the body, ye shall live."

II. HERE'S WHAT'S HAPPENING NOW FOR YOUR HEALING

Please read John 5:1-9 and then follow me step by step into getting yourself in position for better health —and, yes, miracle-living after your healing.

First, there were a lot of people at the pool at Bethesda in Jerusalem because they were ill in some way, and because they believed in the legend of the angel boiling up the water so that the first one to get in would be cured of whatever ailment he had.

It was pretty exciting to have a try at the waters that supposedly carried healing in them.

Well, a lot of people today are ill—in fact, I believe everybody is sick in *some way*.

You are. I am. Everybody is. Sickness takes different forms in the body, or the mind, or the spirit, or in our relationships, or in our attitude. Especially in our attitude, or the way we look at things and act in that way.

Second, this particular man waiting at the pool for his cure was apparently not organically ill. He could be described today as being *psychosomatically* ill. This kind of illness, if that is what he had, is said to spring from the emotions and is often dismissed as, "Oh, it's only in his mind."

If that *is* what it was, then he was in bad shape because it's just about impossible to cure it with medicine or surgery. Prayer has a hard time with it too. For God must get *inside* the person, and for that to happen the person must *will* it to be.

Now we are dealing with something deeper than the mind and more powerful than the body—the human spirit. How *strong* you are in your spirit! Strong because that is the essence of your being. That's the part with which you start your contact with God who alone can successfully deal with you in your inner self.

If, as is reported, some 85 percent of our illnesses are emotionally induced, then understanding how to RISE UP IN YOUR SPIRIT (the inner man standing up in your body) is about the most important thing you must learn.

Of course I believe God, through the power of prayer, can heal organic diseases too—those illnesses that originate in the body itself, or a combination of the body and emotions.

But I've discovered that in praying for many thousands of different people, it's difficult to know the difference between organic and psychosomatic illness. Doctors have told me they don't always know. Some, like a broken limb, are pretty clearly organic; some, like arthritis, may or may not be—it isn't easy to know.

Personally I think *the key issue* for a doctor or one praying for a healing is to accept all healing as coming from God—or putting first things first. In other words, know that all healing is divine no matter what delivery system is used to bring it.

This gets us out of the area of fragmenting God's ways of healing. We don't say just prayer alone, or just medicine alone, as if the two are incompatible, or that both are not delivery systems God freely uses.

The first physician to make the famous statement, "I cut; God heals," knew what he was talking about. The Bible that says, "The prayer of faith shall save the sick, and the Lord shall raise him up" (James 5:15) is absolutely correct. Whichever method God uses in healing is good and acceptable—and more power to both!

Third, the pool of water seemed to be the wrong instrument for this man whose illness had brought him there over a space of 38 long years. For when Jesus walked up and looked at him, He saw inside his being and located the real healing problem. His spirit was wrong. "Will you be made a whole person?" Jesus asked.

The man had his mind on his illness and the possibility of the boiling water of the pool of Bethesda recovering his body. It had not become part of his thinking that he himself, his total self, was involved, that action toward healing would have to begin within his spirit—and his will.

We are brainwashed from childhood up that we are mental and physical beings. We are taught that we either are not a spirit at all, or if we are it's not an important part of our being human. So our mind has been elevated above our spirit and has supremacy over our total being. Education as we know it today deals mostly with our mind, not with our spirit. Exactly opposite to the way God created us and intends for us to learn, to love, and to build our attitude and make our decisions.

The Spirit of God and your human spirit must recognize each other. God's Spirit does know you to be a spiritual being and that *all your problems are spiritually based.* Does your spirit know that? Does your spirit take charge over your mind and body and determine to respond to the Holy Spirit? Do you realize inside your intellectual and physical self there is an inner man— —your spirit? Your real self?

Jesus starts with you as He created you—in your spirit, the real you. He asks, "Will *you* be made whole?"

You! Whole! Two key words, two key understandings of who and what you are.

Jesus indicates *when any part of you is ill YOU ARE ILL.* That's true when it's psychosomatic or organic or both. You, the person, are affected all through yourself. Therefore, He starts with your *will.* Your will operates through your mind and body but originates in your inner man, your spirit.

This is why I believe:

> NOBODY IS EVER FULLY HEALED, RE-
> GARDLESS OF HOW SUCCESSFUL
> MEDICINE MAY BE, OR SURGERY MAY BE,
> OR PRAYER MAY BE, UNTIL HE WILLS
> IN HIS SPIRIT FIRST—LETTING IT WORK
> UP THROUGH HIS MIND AND BODY—
> TO BECOME A WHOLE PERSON.

Fourth, when Jesus asked the man if he willed to be made whole he replied, "Sir, I have no man, when the water is troubled (boiling up), to put me into the pool!"

He had what I call "tunnel vision." I've had it so often that I know pretty well what it is and how it can negatively affect you in getting better health, or in seeing life as a whole.

Tunnel vision was like he was looking through a tunnel and all he could see at the other end was that one instrument—the pool of water—and he hoped he would get in first. He had failed for 38 years. How long have you failed by having tunnel vision?

I just wish we could put all of God's delivery systems of healing and health where they belong—*in Him.* Because we can know God and through our spirit will to be whole, we don't have to be limited by medicine alone, as tunnel vision; or by prayer alone, as tunnel vision—or anything else, as tunnel vision. To get away from the hindrances of tunnel vision we see God as the total Source. These other things we see as vital and necessary instruments. This can put you in a position to know GOD CAN MAKE A WAY WHERE THERE SEEMS TO BE NO WAY.

Fifth, Jesus was very aware of the man's suffering body, but He began the healing process by talking to him concerning his down spirit—of getting it to respond first. The man inside—the inner self—the central core of our existence as a human which was made in God's image and likeness. Jesus knew this man had completely overlooked this. Jesus saw a *person* inside the body, and that inner person was lying down. Still the man wanted his body healed. He simply had not recognized that Jesus was concerned about his whole person, and it had to begin in his spirit.

WHAT A PHYSICIAN TOLD ME

A top physician told me recently that medical and surgical help could be many times more consistent and longer lasting IF they could get people to understand there is something about them that is more than physical, and something more involved in their recovery than what doctors or therapy can do for them. He said that physicians use medical, rather than theological, terms because that is their training and expertise; but they all know the healing process takes on a new dimension when something INSIDE THE SICK PERSON BEGINS TO FUNCTION.

I shared with him this encounter Jesus had with the man at the pool, how Jesus began with his spirit and will, and finally by coming right out and telling him to do three things:

RISE,

TAKE UP YOUR BED,

AND WALK.

He asked me to explain that, to see if there was any relationship to what he had just told me. Here is what I said:

RISE.

The man's body carried in it an illness that made him weak or unable to function as one involved in normal life. He blamed others for getting in his way and preventing him his chance to plunge into the so-called healing waters. He was frustrated and full of inner conflicts over it. He seemed to be quite bitter too. He blamed everybody but himself.

Isn't it better for us to accept responsibility? Isn't it also better to be frank and get out of our system bad thoughts by speaking them out: "I am bitter." "I don't like my doctor." "Nobody is praying for me." "Everybody is against me." If you feel any of these, you should speak them out of your system and ask forgiveness of God.

Then you can begin with your spirit and speak forth positive healing thoughts such as: "I am a person of worth and God loves me." "God wants me to will to be well." "My doctors are for my health." "My friends are praying that I will be restored and I am praying for them as a seed I plant." "God is my Source of healing." "God can make a way for me where there is no way." "I believe it."

It's in this way you cause yourself to stand up on the inside. Your spirit is no longer down.

When this happens, how happy your doctor and family will be. Those praying for you will be encouraged to believe that even a miracle can happen to you. There's a better chance that you'll make it.

Your spirit being UP makes all the difference in the world in your life.

WHEELCHAIR VICTIMS

In the lay seminars which we have several times each year here at Oral Roberts University, we take the closing day for the time to specifically pray for each one to be healed. I have spent a lot of time from the opening night (there are four days) talking about learning how to see yourself as being a spirit with a mind and body which completes you as a human being. I talk about the Miracle of Seed-Faith, how God gives us three miracle keys to get our needs met.

> *One*, make God your Source (Philippians 4:19), "But my God shall supply all your need . . . " God, not any body or any thing—just God using *different instruments* and *delivery systems*.

Two, give, and it shall be given unto you (Luke 6:38). This means, plant a seed of faith first in order to receive, or reap, a harvest (Matthew 17:20).

Three, expect a miracle or a harvest in due season (Luke 6:38; Galatians 6:9).

THEN a seed is planted to produce a harvest. The eternal law of sowing and reaping first given by God in Genesis 8:22 will never fail. Jesus' teaching you to give that it shall be given to you, likewise will never fail. However, you must expect a miracle so you will recognize it when God sends it and reach out your hand and receive it.

I emphasize that God did something first—He made His love an act of giving, a seed He planted, by giving His only begotten Son to die on the cross for us—the desired result being our salvation (John 3:16). Therefore, to plant our seed it means *our* love must first become an act of giving. Giving of ourselves in the form of time, money, concern, etc. It must be a true expression—cheerfully given—of our heart.

Now to wheelchair victims: On that last day when everyone in the seminar comes forward for healing prayer, there are usually several people who are in wheelchairs or on crutches. I make no difference between people who are ill and can walk, or people who are ill and can't. Why? Because when you are sick you feel that your sickness is just as bad as that of others, it hurts and hinders you so much.

However, I say something different to people who can only get along in a wheelchair: "You have been in that wheelchair for some time, maybe years. It's good you have something like that to carry you. If it's your intention and your will to come out of it through prayer, then you must *do something first*. For example, *if you can move any part of your body, do it—if it's only a finger or a toe*. Deep inside is your spirit, your inner person. Your spirit is the only one who can cause your inner man to respond. The medicine you are on does certain things for your body, but it will do much more if you respond to healing through your spirit. By responding through your spirit first, your mind will feel the stimulation, including the faith of your soul, and your body is much more likely to feel it too.

"If you just sit there, moving nothing, making no effort, usually nothing will happen. Remember, your body has no will of its own; it's like an inert mass. Therefore, when we touch you in a moment of prayer, DO SOMETHING. You may not be able to get out of the wheelchair through our prayer, or even move much. But your spirit has responded, some help will come to your body as a result of it, and it may be you will RISE from the wheelchair and start getting well! Or at least well enough to walk."

To those who are mobile I urge them, in a different way, to do something. Maybe touch someone else as we touch them, to transfer their entire thought from the intellect of the head to the inner self of the spirit.

This is something I do all the time. If I start with my head first I know I have bypassed my spirit, and thus I have effectively cut off my spirit's response to God. On the other hand, I have not neglected my intellect by responding first with my inner self—my spirit—because then I let that response flow up into my intellect AND into my physical being. That's how I get into the whole-man response.

It's the most powerful method I've discovered. I believe Jesus used it. I believe St. Paul did. I know it works many miracles.

It's really a seed you are planting. You are doing something. You are acting from your inner being, then with your whole self toward God.

The physician I referred to is often with me in the healing service of the seminars. He and I both have been amazed at the high percentage of people coming out of wheelchairs, some after five or ten years or more, and walking!

Some just look at me as if expecting me to heal them. I cannot heal, nor can a doctor, any more than a farmer can grow a crop. The farmer can sow, water, cultivate but only God can make seed multiply into a harvest.

I say, "Move something." I say, "Let your spirit tell your mind and body you determine to be whole by the power of God." I say, "If you can't get up you've lost nothing, for you haven't been able to get up." I say, "Who knows what good will start in you if you move something by faith?"

Well, some move a little and drop back into the wheelchair. I say, "That's no disgrace; you tried. Maybe it will inspire you to try again." Or I say, "Perhaps God has someone else to pray for you, or He has a specialist who can help." Or, "If you are in that chair the rest of your life, you can still accomplish much by remembering to respond first through your spirit."

Then it never fails to happen. A person in a wheelchair will move a finger, a foot, or something. They make an effort to get up. Sometimes the hands tremble or the body shakes as it is unaccustomed to movement. A foot touches the floor, then the other. A hand is given to steady them. That first step is the hardest.

Then—and every time I see this I glow inside—the light dawns in the eyes mirroring the soul: "I am up. I am taking a step."

Then they turn loose, the body comes alive; bones that have creaked or been lifeless feel life and there they go! A shout goes up. The individual walks, sometimes runs! He bends over, turns sideways, back and forth, gathering new faith, hope, expecting.

Later we get a letter: *I am well!*

That takes your breath away. That tells you something. Especially a year later when he may come to another seminar and with your own eyes you see him well!

Do they all rise and walk? I've never seen it happen except in one of the seminars. Of the 20 or more in wheelchairs, they all got up— they rose and walked, as Jesus said. Whether they all kept it, I don't know; I do know some did. But they all rose up! They got a start and that's important.

The same is true in medicine and surgery. Amazing miracles happen. They are doing things now that once we never dreamed possible. However, despite the skill and the new drugs, without the person being ready, cooperating with all their forces—spirit, mind, and body—these medical miracles just don't seem to happen very often.

In fact, when I see a medical miracle—and I see more and more of them—I know God is on that case, with or without the conscious knowing of those who are the instruments. How can this be? Well, when you touch the eternal laws of God's healing process—medically, through prayer, or other aids—these laws work God's miracles! They always have, they always will.

RISE!
TAKE UP YOUR BED!
WALK!

I further explained to my physician friend about this man whose story is in John 5, that attitude is all-important. He said, "I couldn't agree more." He gave me several illustrations of how a person's strong attitude made an apparently improbable recovery possible through surgery, a medical wonder. He told of some who by all rights should have recovered, or at least improved, but didn't. He said, "As I attend the ORU seminars, and we share together, I am seeing more and more that our success as physicians, and yours as an evangelist, have the same basis. The inner man and his response to our treatment and our care are absolutely necessary."

I said, "Watching you doctors work with people, I notice you *do something* as well as talk to them—and you also have the sick person to *do something*. I encourage you in this, because finding healing and health again starts by both the doctor and the sick person *doing something*. That may be an over-simplification but it's true." He replied that he had never heard it explained in these terms but he had expressed it with many people he had treated.

JESUS SAID, "THOU ART MADE WHOLE!"

Those are cheering words to me. In spite of the fact none of us has ever found the perfect way to help all we seek to help, that we suffer failures again and again, still Jesus' words, "Thou art made whole," convey the possibility of being made whole to each of us.

There is a making process Jesus uses. "Made" whole, is what He says. There's much involved in that, not the least of which is taking advantage of all God's delivery systems. It's using our will as well as our faith. It's responding to our physician and to prayer. It's knowing our spirit is the best "*responder*" we have in order to get our mind and body moving toward being made whole.

I AM LEARNING ABOUT BEING A WHOLE PERSON

Here are some enormously helpful things you can say to yourself:

1. I'll start my journey to wholeness by believing GOD CAN START MAKING A RESTORATION IN MY LIFE.

2. Jesus looks at me with the faith that I can be *made* a whole person out of my dis-ease.

3. Whole is something my faith can "make" me.

4. A spiritual "rebirth" can start me toward wholeness.

5. My wholeness is God's idea.

6. All my problems are spiritually based— therefore, I will receive Christ into my life so I can begin to respond to all of life first through my spirit, then through my mind and body—a whole-man response to life.

TODAY I AM A NEW CREATURE IN JESUS CHRIST (2 Corinthians 5:17).

NOW FOR MY HEALING . . . RESPONDING TO GOD THROUGH MY SPIRIT

7. Understanding how to RISE UP IN MY SPIRIT (my inner man) is the most important thing I must learn.

8. I believe that ALL healing is divine regardless of the delivery system God uses to bring it.

9. I will understand Jesus is asking me: "Will you be made whole?"

10. I believe God will make a way where there seems to be no way.

 key issue: **Responding To God Through My Spirit Puts Me In A Better Position To Be Healed In My Total Being**

The next chapter is powerful in showing you a way to constant better health and better life in every part of your being...

Chapter 6

YOU ARE A SPIRITUAL BEING AND THE SAVING OF YOUR SOUL IS YOUR WHOLE LIFE RESPONDING TO GOD

 key issue: **My Whole Life Can Respond To God ... It Starts In My Spirit**

You reach God through your soul and it is through your soul that God reveals himself and gives life to your total being.

Remember that when God breathed the breath of life into man's body man became something more powerful, more valuable, and more responsible than any other living creature. He became "a living soul." He was God's masterpiece.

It was this inbreathing of God's own spiritual and moral likeness into the physical body of man that caused him to become a spiritual being. Because that is the way God made him, it is so important for you and for me to respond to life *first through our spirit.* Being a spiritual being we must respond from what we are.

Jesus declared to the woman at the well in Samaria, who was a sinner, "God is a Spirit: and they that worship him must worship him in spirit" (John 4:24).

In spirit.

God who is Spirit made you like himself; therefore, your soul, your spirit or your inner man, must govern your physical and intellectual life. In this way that governing is a whole-man governing and it's the whole-man approach that lifts you to the highest of health and success in this life.

RESPONDING WITH YOUR SPIRIT

Look, and listen to a stringed musical instrument responding or reacting to the touch of human fingers and the fingers responding to what the fingers feel from the inner self of the player—just so, your body and your mind respond or react to the force from within you, that vital life-force God calls your S-O-U-L.

A person's mind can create and set in motion many wonders, his body can help bring them into being. But the inner self, the spirit, is the real guiding force so that what the mind and body do—for good or for bad—is first received from the inside.

"In spirit," Jesus said.

At Oral Roberts University we have music students who can play all kinds of instruments, including stringed ones. At a musical recital I watched a young man playing the violin. I was fascinated by the remarkable sounds, the harmony, the beauty. From where I sat it seemed the violin was responding only to the touch of his human fingers. But I realized behind his fingers and hand was something much more important and that was the countless hours of practice in learning the mechanics, and back of that was the imprint of his professor upon his spirit to understand that piece of music, and back of it all was the inner man or spirit translating itself to the fingers, to the strings, to the entire instrument, and presto! beautiful music to calm and uplift us.

YOUR SPIRIT CAN AWAKEN

A person can awaken inwardly to the moving of the Spirit while quite young. "Remember now thy creator in the days of thy youth, while the evil days come not" (Ecclesiastes 12:1). Through a combination of needs I felt as a 17-year-old boy, my spirit awakened and directed my mind and body into repentance of my sins and to be born again. I prayed the sinner's prayer, "Lord, be merciful to me a sinner," and believed in my heart that God received me, and He did. It is from this beginning when I was but a youth that I continually renew myself daily in the Spirit to help me be a good disciple, or follower, of my Savior Jesus Christ.

I am on the stairsteps. Sometimes I trip and fall back a step or two but I always get up and start climbing again. The important thing to me is that I am on the stairway; I am climbing and someday I'll be at the top with God forever. I will be able to go through death and the resurrection, living forever as a whole person. The new birth started all that for me.

A person can awaken to his need of the new birth in his early or middle years. Many do. Or in his mature years as my 84-year-old friend did. I like to say, "It is never too late." And I always add, "But it is later than you think."

If you are already saved and know you are born again, take your pen and write, "I know I am born again by Jesus Christ, my Savior and my Source."

_____

Signed

On the other hand, if you do not know but want to know you are born again, I earnestly suggest you go back and read again the first important *step* in Chapter 3, page 48. Then when you feel in your spirit that Christ is coming alive in you, take your pen and write, "I am being born again today by the Lord Jesus Christ, my Savior and my Source."

_____
Signed

 My Whole Life Can Respond To God ... It Starts In My Spirit

Chapter 7

HOW PRAYING WITH YOUR SPIRIT AND YOUR UNDERSTANDING WILL BRING YOU INTO CONSTANT BETTER HEALTH

 key issue: **My New Relationship With God Has A Language All Its Own**

Tongues, or what I call THE PRAYER LANGUAGE OF THE SPIRIT, is a very important contribution God enables you to make to your better health.

I personally know this to be true. I had spoken in "tongues" shortly after my conversion and a few times since but I never understood how valuable it was to my overall well-being as a person.

It was in a period of deep stress that I was praying and asking God to help me. I was walking by myself on the open field where God had told me to build Him a university. As I walked I prayed and there was no living thing visible but the rabbits and squirrels and birds. I was trying to pray but the words were sticking in my throat or seemingly were being hurled back at me.

As my distress grew I felt something deep inside me, stirring. Suddenly a warm sensation of His presence flooded upward and words came to the tip of my tongue, words I could hear, but words that were not of my own creation or understanding.

By previous experience I knew it was "other tongues," as spoken of in the lives of the early Christians in New Testament times. I let them flow out of my mouth as I spoke them. As before, in the few times I had spoken in tongues, I felt a sense of relief and release in my spirit. But it wasn't enough to feel better, now I had to *know* something I didn't know. I was in desperate need to do what God had called me to do; build Him a university, building it on His authority and on the Holy Spirit. Plus, I had to build it academically sound, properly funded, and in a way to educate the *whole* man. That was God's command to me.

Frankly, my intellect was staggering under the load of this mammoth undertaking. I felt terribly unprepared.

By a divine prompting—or by what some might call a coincidence—when I finished saying these words in "other tongues" I started right in praying in my own language again. But wait a minute, *something was different.* The words coming out of my mouth in English were not the same as I had been using just before I spoke with tongues. These words, although in English, had a message for my mind. God was speaking back to me; He was enlightening me. My intellect was coming alive in a new way. What I didn't know until two or three days later was I WAS INTERPRETING MY OWN TONGUES BACK TO MY UNDERSTANDING.

I knew this was in 1 Corinthians 14:13, where St. Paul said, "Let him that speaketh in an unknown tongue pray that *he* may interpret." (Not someone else, but himself do the interpreting.)

The thing that was happening as I walked and prayed in my own understanding of the impossible challenge God had given me, was that I could not work my way through the limitations of my own mind. My intellect could not grasp or understand how to do what God has said. It was beyond my mental powers and human ability.

Now as I prayed in tongues it was "my spirit praying" and reaching out to God. The Holy Spirit in my spirit was helping my inadequacy and inability to get my prayer through to God and to get understanding back. Suddenly I realized this new tongue in which my spirit was speaking to God was in reality a new PRAYER LANGUAGE; a prayer language unknown to my mind, unknown in the sense that my *mind* did not have the ability to know my inner self as my *spirit* did. Before that, it had been more of an intellectual prayer, my intellect creating the words of the prayer. My mind was unable to solve the problem I was facing. The answer to it lay in my spirit. Unknowingly, I had been failing to respond first with my spirit to this challenge that had been laid upon me, rather I was attempting to pray it through with my mind and it wouldn't work. I just wasn't getting any answers by praying with my intellect alone. When I resumed praying in English I was actually intepreting God's responses to what my spirit, by the power of the Holy Spirit, had said to God in tongues which of course were incomprehensible to my mind. In other words, my spirit had bypassed my mind, and by the help of the Holy Spirit who knew exactly how to help me reach God, was using my tongue as the vehicle of expression to God so I could better get His response to the know-how I needed.

I was accustomed to having my mind use my tongue when I talked or prayed. Now I was learning that my spirit could speak through my tongue, independent of my mind or intellect.

But the really important thing was that something was happening to my mind THROUGH THE INTERPRETATION I had made. I guess I just stumbled on to it. In the flash of a second after the interpretation of what I had said in tongues—or the prayer language of the Spirit—my mind opened up with a new understanding. It was able to grasp that through God, I, the least likely one to build Him a university, could do it.

It was like my mind was being watered and cultivated, growing and blossoming, and becoming fruitful. It was bursting with new knowledge. Now I was praying with the understanding. That was the fruit.

THE TONGUE OF UNDERSTANDING

The tongues with interpretation back to my mind gave me THE TONGUE OF UNDERSTANDING.

The next day I tried this again. Evelyn, my darling wife, heard me and said to herself, *all these years Oral has been so balanced, now he's gone off the deep end.*

She changed her opinion, however, when she saw the strain was gone from my face, and became aware of the knowing that had come into my mind. Then I was able to share with her this understanding I now had on how to build the university—from point zero!

Soon she was off alone praying, asking God to release the "prayer language" in her spirit. It happened so beautifully to her. Then I taught her to interpret back to her understanding. I did this by telling her the moment she finished praying in the *prayer language of the Spirit* to immediately start in English, saying what came. She was delighted to see that what her spirit had said to God in tongues was now made clear to her through words of her mind, also God's response came into her understanding. In this way we would be able to pray exactly as St. Paul prayed:

"I will pray with the spirit (in tongues),
and I will pray with the understanding
also" (1 Corinthians 14:15).

From that time on Evelyn and I have been praying in the two-way prayer method Paul used so successfully in his life and work. First in tongues, then with the interpretation back to our mind, enabling us immediately to pray with the understanding also.

Soon I began to understand that the real meaning of "tongues" is more than an inner release of one's spirit and more than receiving a personal blessing (edification). I had once thought that's all it was. But now I know it is also the enlightening of the mind so it can understand and *pray with the tongue of understanding*. I want to tell you that this has been the most helpful aid to my mind I have ever discovered. I am humbly grateful to God for it.

ST. PAUL'S EXPLANATION

In 1 Corinthians 14:14, St. Paul says, "If I pray in an unkown tongue, my spirit prayeth, but my (mind) is unfruitful." First, Paul says "tongues" is praying with our spirit. Next, he says praying with our spirit alone leaves our mind unfruitful, or lacking in understanding of the meaning of the tongues, or God's response to the tongues. Praying only in tongues *does not* accomplish its full mission. But praying in tongues, followed by our interpretation, aids our mind to pray WITH THE UNDERSTANDING ALSO. That's the importance of it.

It's apparent that St. Paul wanted to go beyond the limitations of the mind by beginning his prayer with his spirit (in tongues) by the help of THE HOLY SPIRIT WITHIN HIM. In this way his spirit would speak directly *to* God (1 Corinthians 14:2). He wanted the Holy Spirit to search out his spirit for all the hangups, the inabilities, the inner conflicts, and any other hindrance to a full response to life through his spirit. He knew that the Holy Spirit knew the mind of God and what the will of God is for one's life; therefore, that's where he started his prayer, with his spirit (or in tongues).

Finally, he knew through the prayer language, the Holy Spirit would intercede for him—or us as we use the prayer language—according to God's will. Believe me, this is wonderful!

Paul also knew that he had to follow his prayer in tongues with interpretation of the tongues back to his mind so he could pray with the understanding ALSO. The key to his praying successfully was to get in position to pray with his understanding. The tongues with interpretation helped him to do that.

This is what happened to me that day back in 1961 as I walked and prayed over the barren ground on which God wanted His university to rise. I thank God it has continued every day since. Daily, I pray first in tongues using my prayer language, then I follow it with interpreting back to my mind to make it fruitful and give it understanding. Therefore, you can see that tongues are not an end in themselves, rather they lead to interpretation of God's response to our spirit, enabling us to pray with the mind in understanding. It brings an inner release but if that's all it is, it wouldn't be enough. Praying with the understanding is what tongues are really all about. That is their highest purpose. That's why I value them so highly and use them every day.

Evelyn does the same thing. So do my associates and most of the ORU students. It is a continuous learning process in which we start with our spirit, then follow with the understanding deepened and increased as we follow tongues by interpretation by praying more effectively in our own language. I had to have this "extra" understanding and I have to have it more every day. I am so insufficient within my own knowledge that only as I pray with BOTH my spirit and my understanding am I able to understand and do what God has called me to do.

I believe it is in this spirit that Paul said, "I would that ye all spake with tongues" (1 Corinthians 14:5). He personally knew the value to one's intellect (of praying first in tongues) and of blossoming it to better pray with the understanding.

Perhaps you have never understood tongues, or even heard of it. However, you do know how difficult it is to know how to pray with your mind only, don't you?

One thing that will help you is to know that the Holy Spirit is the invisible unlimited form of Jesus Christ himself. As such, the Holy Spirit live IN you. The Holy Spirit is in your spirit, and your body is the temple or house (1 Corinthians 6:19,20). Think of the Holy Spirit as a person being inside you—you are joined together—now. The Holy Spirit in your spirit creates this new language pattern called tongues, or what I call *the prayer language of the Spirit* (1 Corinthians 14:13-15).

A DREAM STARTED ME

The first time I spoke in tongues was in a dream. The reason I think is because I was inhibited. Tongues were so foolish to my mind. Why should I say things in a language I never had learned? Why should I speak words my mind didn't know the meaning of? That inhibited me? Had I not been inhibited about this I could have used the prayer language the very instant the Holy Spirit gave me the new birth. How do I know this? Well, I know it because I remember the Spirit was flooding up from my inner self, coming up to my tongue. I could easily have opened my mouth and spoken by my spirit . . . had I known. No one taught me and the opportunity passed.

One night I awakened with words of a new tongue on my lips. Although I felt a release in my spirit I didn't know the meaning of what I was doing.

Later, while praying with some Christians who spoke in tongues, I was able to speak a little, a few words only. Still, I did not receive the full benefit because these folks did not interpret back to their understanding, being content with the inner release they felt in their spirit. Apparently that is all they knew about this dynamic, God-ordained experience.

The few times I spoke in tongues again were in moments of deep joy in the Lord, or in moments of deep distress. It was at a high or a low level of my spirit. It was more of a spontaneous speaking rather than by my will. Since I was not taught nor had I learned any more about this experience, I made little effective use of tongues for years. I knew it was scriptural—and I defended it. I only wish I'd understood it better.

Then in 1961, faced with God's mighty challenge to build an impossible university and tie it into the healing power He had called me to take to my generation, the incident of walking across the open field that I have already related, occurred. As I indicated, the tongues came up. There they were. Because of my urgent need, my inhibitions were gone. I have often wondered if my need to understand had not been so great, would I ever have overcome my inhibitions to completely open myself to the prayer language? I remember that as I was praying I urgently wanted to pray from the depths of my being. I was not thinking about praying in tongues but I was completely open to God. No inhibitions in my mind. I merely *willed* to pray, really pray. Then as naturally as I breathed, from my spirit the tongues came over my tongue. Just as naturally I could stop by my will and begin again in my own language.

After the interpretation came and I could follow it by prayer with the understanding also, from that time on I have *chosen* and *willed* to use the prayer language at any moment—I can, and I do.

I can pray in tongues at will or cease at will. It is under my will, not my emotions. Always, I follow tongues by interpreting back to my mind, and then I pray with the understanding. This gives me THE TONGUE OF UNDERSTANDING which is priceless in helping me better respond to God and to do what I am to do with my life. I can't begin to tell you how much this contributes to my general health, and well-being as a person and as a Christian. When I pray in tongues I direct it toward a need or a goal, then interpret back God's response to my mind and follow it by praying in English with real and deep understanding. If this seems impossible, I can only tell you it *is* possible. If it seems strange, I can assure you once you do it and keep on doing it, it will be as natural as breathing—and as important.

BETTER HEALTH

In the overall life I am living, I know beyond all doubt this prayer power aids my health because when both my spirit and mind are reintegrated I am more in harmony with my total self—spirit, mind, and body. I believe God has this charismatic aid for every child of God. Indeed, I believe it is already in him waiting for his *choosing* and his *will* to release it. We may have different callings but this precious aid to our praying is available to all of us as we need it, which to me is often. I've never seen anyone—I mean anyone—fail to receive the prayer language who really *chose* and *willed* to have it from God, especially when they had some guidance from one who uses it whom they trust in the Spirit.

There's better health ahead and God wants us to "be in health . . ." (3 John 2).

Now, some helpful self-starters:

PRAYING WITH MY SPIRIT
AND MY UNDERSTANDING
WILL BRING ME INTO BETTER HEALTH

1. The PRAYER LANGUAGE OF THE SPIRIT is a very important contribution I can make to my better health.

2. It is my choice and my will to pray in the spirit.

3. Praying in the spirit and interpreting back to my mind helps renew my mind (Ephesians 4:23). Therefore, I will pray WITH THE TONGUE OF UNDERSTANDING (1 Corinthians 14:15).

 key issue: ***My New Relationship With God Has A Language All Its Own***

A SUMMARY OF STEP NUMBER ONE...

Things I Must Do And Remember In My New Relationship With God:

key issue: 1. **I WILL PUT FIRST THINGS FIRST** *by studying the Scripture so I can receive the greatest miracle of my life — my salvation.*

key issue: 2. **I AM AWARE OF MY NEED FOR A NEW LIFE** *so I can be open to the healing of my whole person.*

key issue: 3. **I AM ON THE ROAD TO A NEW LIFE AND BETTER HEALTH** *because God is my Source and my Savior.*

key issue: 4. **MY NEW LIFE WITH GOD CAN START WHERE I AM RIGHT NOW** *and regardless of my age, I can be born again by saying, "Lord, be merciful to me, a sinner."*

key issue: 5. **MY WHOLE LIFE RESPONDS TO GOD, IT STARTS IN MY SPIRIT.** *Now that I have received Christ as my Savior and Source, my spirit is responding to His life, and I am on the stairway to becoming a disciple of JESUS CHRIST.*

key issue: 6. **RESPONDING TO GOD THROUGH MY SPIRIT PUTS ME IN A BETTER POSITION TO BE HEALED IN MY TOTAL BEING.** *"Wholeness" is something my faith can bring to me.*

key issue: 7. **MY NEW RELATIONSHIP WITH GOD HAS A LANGUAGE ALL ITS OWN.** *Praying in the prayer language means that I can get through to God at any time and it can bring me into constant better health.*

TWO

**Your life will be completely
different *if* you learn to plant
good seed with God and
with people you like or dislike.**

Chapter 1

WHEN YOU DON'T LIKE GOD YOU ARE REALLY SAYING YOU DON'T LIKE ALWAYS TO RECOGNIZE GOD AS YOUR SOURCE

 key issue: **I Will Look To God Alone As My Source And Not To People**

Every time I have felt impressed to do something for God that involves heavy financial costs, I have never had any money to start with.

Through the years of this ministry I inwardly knew the time would come to build a university to educate the whole man. This was to be an integral part in fulfilling God's call to take His healing power to my generation. It wasn't easy to see but I knew God would make it plain if I could listen and understand.

God had said, *"Build Me a university. Build it on My authority and on the Holy Spirit."* Then He added, *"Raise up your students to hear My voice, to go where My light is dim, where My voice is heard small, and where My power is not known, even to the uttermost bounds of the earth. Their work will exceed yours and in this I am well pleased."*

I began to see that my call to take His healing power to my generation would not end with me, and that it was to extend to future generations through the students.

I HAD A HARD TIME SEEING GOD AS MY SOURCE

God found a willing response in me to obey Him and to take on this tremendous responsibility. What I didn't like was: I had no money, no land, no faculty, no students, and really nobody to back me. I had a hard time seeing God as my Source.

I had looked around and seen nothing and nobody that could be the source from which I could draw on to carry out this project for God.

"Why, God," I asked, "are You asking me to do this when I don't kow how, I don't have the money, and there's no one I can turn to—Why! Lord?"

He reminded me, "No one to turn to? I AM YOUR SOURCE. Give, and it shall be given to you. Start planting a seed of faith for each part of the university and I will multiply it back to cover every need for you."

So what I would do from time to time was to empty my billfold and my associates would volunteer to do the same thing. Often the whole pile lying on the table was no more than two or three hundred dollars. Although a building we were to build was to cost hundreds of thousands of dollars, and we had only a pittance toward it, I gained inner strength from the fact we had planted a seed, although it seemed pitifully small. Then I would immediately get aggressive in my actions and start digging the hole for the foundation of that new building. Digging that hole was very important to the seed I was planting. It was something I was doing in simple childlike faith. That hole was more than a hole, it was my faith being released so I could believe God for miracles.

Let me tell you, we got scared many times. We ran scared. I would reach out in the night hours to God, pleading for help. But God never seemed to be anxious, like I was. I'd get up and read in my Bible how one of His servants would put a seed in and be able to trust Him who is all-powerful and all-knowing. I'd calm down and get some sleep.

The next morning I'd go look at the big machines moving dirt and look at my associates and go away muttering to myself.

Then I'd get to thinking about God, my Source.

"But my God shall supply all your
need according to his riches in
glory by Christ Jesus" (Philippians
4:19).

GOD WAS ALL I HAD BUT I REALIZED THAT INCLUDED HIS RICHES

I'd meet with my associates and we'd talk about this. We drew close together in these hours—and we still do for we're still digging holes; still building.

One day the business manager of the University said, "Oral, the single most powerful idea you have come up with is, MAKING GOD YOUR SOURCE. The more I hear you talk about it and see you trying to do it in building the school and in applying it in other areas of your life in the healing ministry, the more I see it is the key to our success. If we can understand it ourselves and get others to understand HOW TO MAKE GOD OUR SOURCE, it will change everything for them and for each of us here as we launch forth to obey God."

He smiled and added, "Making God our Source will get us out of ourselves and into His hands and we can draw from His riches when we have none of our own — and He will see us through."

We all agreed, but there was still some shakiness among us, especially in me as the leader. I would lead in prayer:

"O God, we have put in our seed, we
have given first as Jesus has said,
and so we undertake this Seed-Faith
project, depending on You as the Source
of our total supply."

I would find an exaltation rising in me: God is my Source! Then later it would die down as the devil whispered, "You'll never be able to build a university. You'll never get the money; besides, people won't believe you."

IT WAS FRIGHTENING

It was frightening and I didn't like to be in a frightened state. Still, I was able to hold on to this great truth that God is our Source of total supply. That became the miracle key to unlock the doors of many hearts, and soon we saw buildings rising which had seemed impossible. We saw faculty coming when the experts had said they wouldn't come. We saw students coming to cast their lot with us when they could have gone to virtually any university in America. And miracle of miracles, God helped us to put the school together and open on time! That was in 1965 and it can never be taken away as the evidence that God IS our Source and He supplies the needs of those who plant their seed and trust in Him for miracles.

Since then the University has found its place in God's healing plan for this ministry. More and more we are learning to take each new phase, such as the School of Medicine, the School of Theology, the School of Law, as another Seed-Faith project—and to start it with whatever seed we can plant, large or small, then immediately start digging the hole and begin construction.

One of Tulsa's most successful businessmen said, "Oral, according to all reason you can't do this. It's impossible. While others who build universities start with getting the funds first, you start with no money but an idea only—it's not logical." Then he said, "But here it is, a full-fledged university known and recognized all over the world. And you're still building!"

I said, "Yes, but you take away our making God our Source, and you take away our putting in the seed first and putting it in out of our need, you take away our expecting miracles from the seeds of faith we sow—take that away and IT IS IMPOSSIBLE."

He said, "Well, it seems to work."

I replied, "It'll work, if we work it as God says in His Word."

THE STRUGGLE CONTINUES

However, I must admit that even now I often find I don't like having to trust God as my Source. My humanness wants to see where everything is coming from. I don't want to launch out in faith alone. I want all that security people talk about.

I have searched the Scripture, I have prayed to God, I have tried other ways and I am completely convinced that Seed-Faith is God's way and it is the only way. First, God's way is for us to make Him the Source of our total supply. Second, God's way for me—for you—is to start everything we do by first *seeding* for a miracle. Third, it is God's way to expect it to happen from His hand. And it does happen in God's own time and way. Every seed we plant has its own "due season" and that's why we must expect it (Galatians 6:9)...*And let us not be weary in well doing: for in due season we shall reap, if we faint not.*

Many times I have said that I may not convince anyone else on seeding for miracles but Oral Roberts is convinced. The beautiful thing is that being convinced in my own heart and sincerely trying to obey God in Seed-Faith, I am seeing it open the minds of thousands to a new possibility. It is causing them to understand they can make it through their own Seed-Faithing to God. They are seeing, as I do, that it never fails.

Of course the way you Seed-Faith to God for your needs may take different forms, since your needs may be different from mine. But the Seed-Faith principle is the same. It will never fail you because it is the eternal principle of God. It goes all the way back to the first book in the Bible, to Genesis 8:22, "While the earth remaineth, seedtime and harvest...shall not cease." Across the centuries and in all situations people who have believed in seedtime and harvest and practiced it, have found God to be faithful to His own divine commitment to us.

DO YOU GET TIRED OF TRUSTING GOD AND DEPENDING ON HIM ALONE?

I wish I could say I never get tired or resentful of trusting and depending on God alone. I wish I could tell you I never have a desire to turn to certain people and make them my Source. But I can't tell you that. I can tell you that I am often tempted to say, "God, You have me so bound to You that I can follow only one path, Yours. I never get my own way. I never get to lay plans of my own making. I always have to come back to Yours."

SEEING EYE DOG

But you know this idea of depending upon a source is found in many areas of life. For example, I received a lot of help from a story a personal friend, Dr. Bryant Kirkland, pastor of a large New York church, told. He told how one day he was on one of those busy thoroughfares in Manhattan. He was about to cross the street when a young woman came up, led by a seeing eye dog. He realized she was blind. When the light changed and people started crossing over he noticed a truck that had stoppped at the red light from the other direction. The truck driver, a big burly fellow, jumped out, ran over to the girl, and said, "Can I help you across the street?"

She said, "Oh, thank you, but no. You see, I've got to trust my seeing eye dog. I have to depend on him. If I depend upon someone else, my seeing eye dog won't guide me."

The man said, "How old is your dog?"

"He's three years old."

"Well, how can he tell when the light changes from red to green?"

"Well, you know a dog can't tell colors," the girl said.

"Then how do you know when to cross the street," he asked.

She replied, "I don't know how my seeing eye dog knows, but he just knows. And he's never failed me."

The man wished her well and started back to his truck. The girl thanked him for his concern and said, "I've gotten across every street and I'll get across this one, thanks to my seeing eye dog that knows how to take care of me."

Who is your source? Who do you trust to guide and take care of you?

Your source has to know you. He has to know the way you are to take His signals. He has to know when and how. God is the true Source for you.

You must know Him and trust yourself to Him. In the final analysis, everything that is not of God is going to break down and fail. Life is going to be changing, flashing red and green like the stop-and-go signals. Because God is the only One who knows, He will never fail. You can trust Him. But like the girl and her seeing eye dog, if you depend on someone or something else, then God won't guide you.

A 21-YEAR-OLD DISCOVERS WHO HIS SOURCE IS

A young man from Atlanta, Georgia, wrote how hard it was for him to discover who his Source is. As a

21-year-old college student, he accepted Christ as his personal Savior. He said he thought of God in terms of the salvation of his soul and when he died he would go to heaven. Meanwhile, he fell in love and after a long courtship he was getting married. One month before the marriage ceremony everything fell apart, and against his will he and the girl broke up.

He wrote, "I was deeply hurt and frustrated. I had worked carefully to put this marriage together and suddenly I was devastated.

"Two days later I came across a copy of your book, *A Daily Guide To Miracles*. I had nothing else to do that morning so about 8 o'clock I began to read. At 4:30 the next morning, with tears in my eyes, I finished and put the book down. What happened to me while reading the book was, I learned what God's love is all about. Jesus who had been my Savior now became much more—a real, living, helping, loving, caring *now Person* to me. Mentally, as I read I began applying the principles of Seed-Faith, particularly on who my Source is. In this short time, by coming to know Christ as Source as well as Savior, it has brought me out from my failure in putting this marriage together and being devastated by it. I feel loved by God. I realize He is in charge of my life. I know He has someone better for me and a better marriage. I have found myself because of the realization that God is my Source."

As I read his letter I remembered some of my experiences before marriage when I, too, was floundering, not knowing God wanted to be my Source. I thought of how this young man had dated this girl until they were engaged to marry. He had blotted out every other girl in the world as a potential wife, and had concentrated only on this one girl. Now it was all over. That can break a young person down, boy or girl.

But he discovered new things about God. God's total concern for him AND THE GIRL. He saw he could give as a seed he planted and his Source would multiply it back in the form of the right girl for him, and right boy for her. He saw God in that light for the first time. So he was able to land on his feet and bounce back, ready and expectant for God, his Source, to supply his needs.

GET AGGRESSIVE ABOUT THIS

The thing I notice about most people I deal with through this ministry who are suffering some form of illness and who are not into miracle-living, is that they are not aggressive about knowing God as their Source. They dare to start when life's red light is flashing and all too often they get hit—unnecessarily. God has a green light too and He knows when it's green and when it's time for you to start your thing.

People think they know how to run their lives but none of us does. Only God knows all things, the end from the beginning. How can we be so foolish as to trust ourselves in the hands of anyone but God?

Of course I believe you have to have spiritual insight for this. It's something I have aggressively sought, and aggressively seek today, to have the spiritual perception on who I can trust as my Source—God!

Many times I've been so foolish in thinking I knew the way, or someone knew it for me, not realizing the all-knowing God inside me is always available and eager to help me.

I believe these thoughts will help you now...

IMPORTANT THINGS TO REMEMBER

1. God is all I have, but that includes HIS riches.

2. When I get scared to trust God as my Source I will say: "God is my Source, God is my Source, God is my Source" . . . and believe it.

3. I will get aggressive about looking to God as my Source.

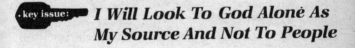

key issue: *I Will Look To God Alone As My Source And Not To People*

Chapter 2

YOU MAY THINK YOU DISLIKE GOD WHEN THE TRUTH IS YOU JUST CAN'T STAND PEOPLE

 key issue: **I Will Pray For People I Like Or Dislike Because God Loves Them All**

Many people are disillusioned about God because they have the wrong information about Him. I encourage anyone who really doesn't like God, to say it. Here's what some have told me:

"God? He doesn't care about anything, certainly not what I am going through. If He cared He would do something about it."

"As far as I'm concerned, I don't want God's name mentioned to me again."

"Where is God? He's never there when I need Him."

"If there is a God, why doesn't He stop all the wars and suffering?"

"Why doesn't God clean up our country?"

"If God is so good, as you say He is, why doesn't He heal my little afflicted child?"

"We're so desperate for money. That's one thing God never seems to notice."

I've heard every one of these statements said about God, and more.

I TOLD GOD TO GET OUT OF MY LIFE

I remember some of the negative things I said about God. Really, I said some of them to God. Once I said, "God, get out of my life." God knew I had come to the point that I meant it and He got out of my life. It was an eerie feeling when I became aware of His seeming unawareness of me, that He was letting me alone.

I told my parents many times when I lay ill with tuberculosis that God didn't care anything about me.

The other day a mother overburdened with her problems, who had seen me on television, met me and blurted out, "Oral Roberts, I don't like your God. Now what do you have to say to that?"

"What do I have to say about your not liking God? Well, I think if you feel that way you should tell Him."

"Well, I've told you."

"Tell *Him*."

"Oh, that would be wrong."

"Why?"

"You know, He's God and I'm just...a...woman."

"Yes, but you are a person made in God's image and likeness. He made you unique and irreplaceable. He loves you very much and wants to..."

Interrupting me she said, "Loves me? Well, if He knew the sickness, the bills piling up, the worry I go through..."

"He knows and He cares. He's been through it and He's the only One who can lead you through it."

"Well, I never heard anyone say that. Most people say you get what you deserve and I don't think I deserve what's happening to me."

I said, "Ma'am, can you realize there's a devil in the world, that he doesn't like you, that the Bible describes his going about as a roaring lion seeking to devour people, that when you are sick or injured or down and out, it is the oppression of the devil that he is trying to put upon you?"

She said, "Is that in the Bible?"

"Yes, ma'am, it's in the Bible," I replied, "and lots more just like it. God wants to prosper you, heal your family, supply your financial needs, give you a closer walk with Him."

Tears came in her eyes. She said, "Oral Roberts, will you pray for me?"

PRAYING ONE FOR ANOTHER

I said, "Yes, if you will pray for someone else as I pray for you."

She said, "I don't know how to pray for someone else. I am so mixed up and hurt I don't know how to pray for myself, let alone anyone else."

I asked her if she knew what it was to pray. She said she guessed she didn't, since she had not prayed much in her life.

I told her what my mother had said prayer was when, as she urged me to pray during my illness, I said I didn't know how to pray. Mamma said, "Oral, you don't have to know how to pray. Just tell God what you feel in your heart. He'll understand and He'll answer."

She asked me how she would know. "You'll know," I said, "you'll just know." I knew that deep within her intuitive self she would know.

The first time I tried to pray I remembered Mamma telling me to tell God exactly how I felt. It was bitterness and disappointment that came out. It was not so nice sounding, I am sure. But I felt a lot better. Later, I asked Him to save my soul and He did! Before that, however, my prayers had nothing in them which indicated I wanted God's help.

THIS MOTHER PRAYED FOR THE ONE SHE LIKED THE LEAST

To the worried and harried mother talking to me, I said, "Can you think of the person you like the least?"

She laughed bitterly, "A lot of them."

"Call off several to me, not by name if you don't want, but their profession or relationship to you."

Tossing her head she said, "I'm behind four months in my rent, how do you think I feel about the man who says we have to move out? And my former husband who's forgotten he ever had children, my children that I love and am working my hands to the bone for. My kinfolks who never come by. My only sister who is well-off but wouldn't help me if her life depended on it." And she went on and on.

"That's great," I said, "to get all that poison out of your system. I have a feeling you feel the worst toward God."

She said, calmed a little by now, "Well, in the back of my mind I've always believed there is a God. But all that hellfire preaching, all that stuff about God's got your number, I really don't know what to think anymore."

I said, "Look at me, please."

When she did, I said, "Listen, you talk and sound about like I did at one time in my life. I didn't like God. I didn't want God. I wanted God out of my life. I thought I could make it without Him. I never prayed or asked for His help. I ended up traveling the last mile of the road with a need so great that no mortal power could meet it, not doctors, not religious doctrines, nothing but GOD HIMSELF GIVING ME A MIRACLE."

"Yes," she said, "I've heard you tell that on TV. Did it really happen? Is it really so?"

I said, "It's really true. Today I breathe because I turned to God. Prayer was the key that unlocked the door. I met God and He met me and I was restored in my being. I'm well today. I know that I know that I know..."

Wiping the tears away, she said, "Oh, Mr. Roberts, if only I could get out of this mess I'm in, I'd do anything."

"You can! There's something you can do. And doing it is very important to you."

I reminded her of the people she liked the least; again I asked her to pray for them as I prayed for her.

PLANT A SEED-FAITH PRAYER

She asked what good that would do. I said, "It's Seed-Faith. You plant a seed by praying for someone else even if you don't like him or he has wronged you. Jesus teaches that if you give, it shall be given to you. He says this in Luke 6:38."

Quickly, she said, "I don't have anything to give."

"Well, you may not have the money to give but you have something in your heart you can say to God to help these you feel have been unkind or neglectful of you. That's a seed, too. Seed is not always money. It can be. Sometimes it's something more important, like a prayer for a person you need to forgive or who needs to forgive you..."

She choked up as we joined hands to pray. "Tell God how you feel about Him," I whispered.

I heard her mumbling a few phrases but they were mostly about her own problems.

Abruptly her voice became steady. She said, "O Lord, I don't know exactly how to say this but I feel in my heart now that I want You to help Mr. _____ , and help my kinfolks, and my former husband . . ." She kept naming off different people whom she had despised. And then she said, "I love God—I just can't stand people."

When she finished, I said, "Don't feel embarrassed ever by doing what you've just done. *In the future when you have other bad feelings, pray this way again. This is Seed-Faith praying, the kind that God multiplies back to you in meeting your needs*: the rent money, healing for your family, a new hope for a better life, a closer walk with God, joy in your heart, becoming a real solid person."

I get letters from this mother quite often and I always pray and write her back, as I do others who write. It is especially gratifying to read her letters when she says:

"I never knew God could be so good."

"I planted another seed and already it has come back three times."

"My oldest child prayed with me last night for the first time."

"My former husband apparently has disappeared completely but God is taking care of my needs."

"I feel so close to God."

"I've learned how to expect miracles... God is so real to me...I know He's going to work everything out in my life and in my family."

The best one was, "Dear Oral Roberts, I've learned the secret of how to get all my needs met through Seed-Faith living and through SEED-FAITH PRAYING ...I keep resentment and bitterness out of my life by praying for others and God is so real to me..."

This lady went from blaming God to trusting Him as her Source. This may seem impossible to you, but remember, "With God nothing shall be impossible" (Luke 1:37). I feel sure you are coming to this place in your thinking and believing...

Now I want to list some things that will be of further help to you:

1. If you think you don't like God...tell Him how you feel.

2. If you don't know how to pray, just tell God how you feel in your heart. He will understand and He will answer.

3. Plant a Seed-Faith prayer by praying for the one you like the least.

You may want to pray something like this:
"O Lord, I don't know exactly how to say this but I feel in my heart now that I want You to help _____, and my relatives...(continue to name the

Chapter 3

HOW A WHOLE CHURCH SOLVED ITS INSIDE PROBLEM OF BITTERNESS

 key issue: **Praying For Someone Else Will Begin A Healing In Me**

Recently I had a free Sunday and called the pastor of a black church who had asked me a long time before to preach at his church, even on short notice. If I would call he would change any plans so his people could hear me. When I called he said, "Come right on. We'll get the word out quick."

When I arrived that Sunday morning the place was filled and people were sitting in the aisles and filling the doorways.

GIVE GOD YOUR BEST THEN ASK HIM FOR HIS BEST

My message was, Give God your best, then ask Him for His best. At the end of the sermon, I did two things: First, I asked everyone there, including myself, to give God their best, and in this instance, "Let it be the biggest money bill you have in your billfold or purse."

I said, "Not because God needs it, although there must be money to do His great work here on earth, but because you have a need of your own." Everyone nodded and a man spoke up right out loud, "Reverend

133

Roberts, I've got a big, big need and nobody can meet it but God."

"Then with that need in mind, give Him your biggest bill today."

The pastor had the people to form a line on each side of the church and they came—men, women, children, entire families. The money filled the offering plates, which had been placed on chairs at the front, and spilled over onto the floor. I watched the people. They came very seriously and the moment they put in their biggest bill, their countenance changed to joy. I had told them:

> "Give God your best,
> then ask Him for His best,
> and start expecting a miracle."

I've never felt such a change in people as I did when they gave of their best and returned to their seats.

Second, I asked everyone to think of the person he disliked the most and as we joined hands to pray the Seed-Faith prayer, he should pray especially for that person.

It took some 20 minutes before this prayer was concluded. I thought of the person I liked the least and got him right out in the open before God and my own eyes. I felt so much better. The audience had never been asked to do this and it took them longer. I waited and watched. I would see a man tremble, a mother bend over in tears, a teen-ager dead serious. Then someone would cry out. It was something very real they were experiencing in praying for someone they didn't like.

When it was over you could feel something so good, so fresh and invigorating, it was like a breath of fresh air flowing into the building.

A WOMAN'S DELAYED RESPONSE

A few weeks later the pastor and I saw each other at another function. Grabbing my hand, he told me about the great results that were still coming in from the service that Sunday. He said, "The Tuesday after you preached, my phone rang. It was a grandmother, a poor but influential woman in our area. She said, 'Pastor, could you come to my house today?' I said, 'Of course, I'll be there as soon as I can.' When I arrived she handed me a $20 bill. 'What's this for?' I asked her. She said, 'When Reverend Roberts asked us to pray for the one we liked least, I could do that. When he said to give God our biggest bill, I knew I had this $20 bill and I knew I wasn't going to give something that big. Well, God has shown me how big my needs are since Sunday and He wants my biggest bill so I can be free to ask Him for His best. I can't wait to give it to you to put right to work for the Lord.'

"She gave it to me and I offered it back, knowing what a sacrifice it was. She said, 'Pastor, that's seed my God will multiply and when it comes back multiplied, my need will be met.' "

The pastor looked at me and said, "Dr. Roberts, God has used you to open our eyes. There's been a lot of hard feelings among people attending our church, both toward black people and white people. It's been like a cancer. Now that's disappearing fast and I can feel it happening. Also, what you didn't know was our plan to build a new sanctuary, our third one because of our great growth. When we all gave our biggest bill, it opened us all up, and money is coming in to build. Best of all, some of my people have told me of new jobs, new offers, and one businessman is going to have to build a whole new plant. The whole spiritual tone of the church is the highest it's ever been."

I thanked him for sharing this with me. It further confirmed my personal experience that it works, not only in a church but in one's individual personal life.

GOD WILL WORK MIRACLES IN YOUR LIFE IF YOU WILL LET HIM

One of the best ways to let God work His miracles in your life, and through you to others, is to get out of your system all the things you don't like about God, so you will get into a positive Seed-Faith relationship with Him.

Talk to God. Tell Him how you feel. You may be surprised to find that you will come into a loving relationship with Him when you begin to talk to Him, because you will find that when you get to *know* Him, you will also know that *He knows how you feel* and wants to help you.

PRAY FOR THOSE YOU DON'T LIKE

Even when you feel there is no good way to personally approach the people you don't like, you can approach them indirectly through God in your prayer to Him for them. This is more effective than you may be able to believe right now, but try it.

God is powerful. He knows how to convey the force of your prayers to the ones you dislike. Even if they never respond to you, your own good feelings inside toward them carries with it a seed of faith which God will never fail to multiply back to you in a harvest of miracles. I mean it, a harvest of miracles back to YOU!

START NOW GIVING GOD YOUR BEST

Won't you consider starting now to give God your best through Seed-Faith prayer, time, talent, money, friendship, and concern, *then asking Him for His best*? It will mean a new life for you in the here and now where your needs are so great.

God has many miracles He hasn't given you yet, many inner healings, many dollars, many friends, many great feelings, and advances for your life.

Listen, friend, I KNOW THE WAY TO BETTER HEALTH AND MIRACLE-LIVING is giving God your best as your constant practice, then with the same aggressiveness of spirit, ask Him for His best AND EXPECT IT. I repeat, AND EXPECT IT. Look for it, for it will not fail to come to you. Looking for it is very important for then you will recognize it and *receive it for your good*.

Say the following to yourself: "It's good to know that I can get out of my system all the things I don't like about God ... so He can give me His better health and fill me with His abundant life."

1. I will say what I feel about God so it will help get me in position to see Him as a loving Heavenly Father to me.

2. I will pray for the people I don't like—this is Seed-Faith praying and it will be multiplied back to me in the form of my need.

 key issue: *Praying For Someone Else Will Begin A Healing In Me*

THE WAY TO MIRACLE-LIVING IS GIVING GOD MY BEST AND THEN ASKING HIM FOR HIS BEST...AND EXPECTING IT SO THAT I WILL RECEIVE IT AS HIS GOOD FOR MY LIFE AND MY LOVED ONES.

Chapter 4

HOW A PERSONAL FRIEND LOST HIS WAY AND FOUND IT AGAIN—AND IF YOU FEEL A LITTLE LOST YOU CAN FIND YOUR WAY TOO

 key issue:

**I Can Live My Life Right
Every Day Through God
My Source And My Strength**

Let me tell you about a very close friend I have in the business world. He and I over the years have helped each other, especially through prayer and exchange of ideas on how God works His miracles.

He is the man who helped me develop an expression I use a lot with people. It's this:

*God works His miracles through people,
not through lightning and thunder and
things like that.*

God acts through people.

God speaks through people.

God expresses himself through people.

*If God acts, speaks and expresses
himself through people, why don't you and
I give Him a great and grand expression
in our lives?*

He has come as near to giving God a great and grand expression in his life as anyone I know. He understands it is through people that God works His miracles, that He is the Source, and that by cooperating with Him He will act and speak and express himself through us as persons and we will personally *experience* His miracles. Also, that we will be instruments of His miracles to others.

In the most practical way he has applied this truth to his family life, his life as a businessman, and to his public life as a member of his state legislature. As a churchman he has contributed of his time and money and ideas. In our ministry he has been a Seed-Faith partner in helping us build Oral Roberts University and carry on this ministry of taking God's healing power to this generation.

HE LOST HIS WAY

In spite of all this he developed some real problems. Recently I learned he had lost his way spiritually. He no longer could pray either with the spirit or with his understanding.* He had lost his Source and was beside himself with tension, frustration, and fear. I am grateful that God let our paths cross in an airport and there he re-experienced miracle-living.

I'll call him Bob although that is not his name, but the story I am about to share with you is true.

Bob had flown to a certain city in his private jet. I was in the small terminal when he walked in and saw me. He said, "Oral, wait a minute. I'd rather see you than any other man in the world."

I said, "Bob, what's wrong?"

He said, "Everything. I'm in trouble."

I knew quite a lot about his life. As a poor boy he

---

*See Step Number 1, Chapter 7 for more on praying with the spirit and with the understanding.

worked his way through college and law school with a great drive to make something of his life. Early he took God into his life, making the important decision to pray before every decision he made, including business. Eventually he had a family, got ahead financially, made a lot of friends and got elected to public office.

One of his goals was to be wealthy and he had a definite financial goal. Two years ago he reached that goal. Then he ran across a man worth twice that much, so without further thought he made that man's worth his goal, raising his sights by 100 percent.

As we sat there in the airport he began talking, pouring out his soul. "Oral, up to that time I was a happy man. I knew God had His hand upon my shoulder, and in every attempt I made in business or public life I prayed for guidance and I believe I received it. Everything I planned and went for was founded on being honest and sincere."

Looking straight at me he continued, "Although I was not called to preach or anything like that, I wanted to be God's man. I yearned to see what God would do with a person of humble origins, who was willing to apply himself and work hard, and who would develop a pattern of giving so that he was sharing what he was and what he earned."

As far as I could see, his life was a testimony that he had done this and was a Seed-Faith man. The people he had helped and the love He had for the Lord and those who worked with him spoke of his honesty, sincerity, and generosity as a committed Christian.

He said, "I'm going to level with you because I believe you will understand and may be able to help me.

I'm becoming troubled in my spirit and for the first time my mind will not work, the deals I'm in are not working out. In fact, I'm on a very big one now and although it's very promising financially, perhaps more than any of my entire life, it is worrying me to death."

"Do you want to share it with me?"

"Yes, very much. I have become connected with a man in a very large business project we are attempting. Usually we make a deal, shake hands, and our word is good. But this man wanted a contract and I gave it to him. It was fair for both sides and I was at peace over it. About three months ago he came back and wanted to water down my part and I did it. A little later he wanted it watered down more and again I did it."

I said, "Why did you water it down? Wasn't it a fair contract?"

"Yes, fair on both sides."

"Well, why did you water it down?"

He said, "Because I am a Christian."

I said, "Why would being a Christian cause you to water down an honest contract?"

"Well," he replied, "I want to win this man to Christ and I felt like if I would give in to him he would respect my Christian experience more."

HIS FIRST AND SECOND MISTAKE

"That's where you made your second mistake," I said.

"My second?"

"Yes, your first was to pattern your financial goals after the man's worth instead of letting God lead you into His goals for you."

Then I said, "Back to your second mistake, here's

what I believe God expects of a Christian. First, you don't go around trying to prove you are a Christian. Next, if you make a fair and honest deal, then that's what it is—honest and fair. You can't change an honest and fair deal without losing your own self-respect, then the respect of the other person. As a Christian you have no right to contribute to the delinquency or dishonesty of anyone with whom you make deals."

He said, "You're right. I see that now. But I'm deeply involved. What can I do?"

I said, "I'll make some suggestions based on the Bible and my own experiences as a Christian who, by virtue of my ministry, has to make business decisions as well as preach the gospel."

He said, "I need to hear them."

I answered, "I suggest you quit being sentimental and emotional about your relationship with this man. Stick with the contract. You are an honest and fair man and you should stand up for the same things you did when you first started with your friend. The only chance you have as a Christian to influence this man for Christ is to carry out the terms of the original contract. Keeping him honest is something he will thank you for; if not now, later. If he doesn't thank you, you have the inner assurance you have fulfilled your word. You have followed the truth of what you believe is right and you can trust God for the results. God will not let you down as long as you hold to the truth."

THERE IS "SOMETHING ELSE"

He said, "I like what you're saying, and although I haven't done it, it's something I had already felt in my heart. But there's something else."

I thought, *there usually is*. It's like when a person gives you all the reasons for not doing something, you say, "Now, what's the real reason?" I've seen that work wonders many times. Then you get down to real facts.

He said, "I've always looked to God as the Source for my life, the Source for my success, but when I got in with this man and saw how wealthy and big he was, I really think I got my eyes on him. And now that he's begun to let me down, I'm losing something out of my life. I don't have the same contact with God."

I listened. He continued, "I really have stopped praying. On the plane coming in here I picked up a Bible and for the first time in several weeks, read something from God's Word."

He looked at me, saying, "Oral, I have forgotten how to pray. Really what I would like most to have from you is a word on how I can start praying again."

I said, "What would you like to say in your prayers?"

"Well, I would like to say to God that I think I've got my mind off Him and onto this man, and maybe I think this man is the one I've been looking to for the success of this deal, the biggest deal of my life, instead of to Him. And I've messed it up."

"Why don't you say that? Why don't you say it to Him as you have said it to me?"

"All right, I'll do it. But I notice on your television programs you ask people to join hands and pray for each other. Would you join your hands with mine, and would you start the prayer?"

Now this was right in the air terminal and people were passing up and down in front of where we were seated. But I knew it was no accident that made our paths cross. My dear friend was oblivious to the crowds—he was doing business with God.

I prayed briefly then asked him if he would speak out of his spirit to God. As he prayed I heard him say with real conviction: "O Lord, remember my friend and bless him. And let him know that I love him." Then he forgot me and kept on praying and soon I saw his eyes fill with tears which were falling down his cheeks and onto the floor. He still had hold of my hands. When he looked up I saw that the strained look on his face was gone. He straightened up, looked around, then said, "Oral, this has been the most exciting moment of my life."

When I asked him why, he answered, "Because as the 23rd Psalm says, He has restored my soul."

We both left, going our separate ways. A friend in his town wrote, "Dear Brother Roberts, what did you do to my friend Bob? He's a completely new man. He's his old self again and going great."

I thought, what did I do? I guess I reminded him of something he already knew and I made him realize that the seeds he had planted, and was planting, were important. That God was his Source and by putting things straight with Him again would cause God to work things out.

This is what you can do if you feel a little lost:

 I Can Live My Life Right Every Day Through God My Source And My Strength

Chapter 5

YOU MAY PANIC WHEN YOU REALLY START PLANTING SEED BY REACHING OUT TO PEOPLE —BUT EVEN WHEN YOU PANIC YOU CAN EXPECT A MIRACLE

 .key issue:

**Even When It Scares Me
I Will Plant Good Seed
By Reaching Out To Others**

My discovery of the term, EXPECT A MIRACLE, hit me right in the middle of a time I was panicking. My life, my ministry, my everything was under physical threats and it appeared I would go down. It happened in the midst of one of our evangelistic crusades.

Many miracles of healing were happening and the news spread near and far. A self-styled atheist took it upon himself to stop the meetings, too many were believing upon Christ as Lord and proclaiming God as the answer to their lives. Threats were made on my life, and each time I went into the pulpit guards were posted and my imagination ran wild. I could almost feel the bullets hitting me. My intellect couldn't shake this off and although outwardly I appeared calm, inside I was afraid. They went so far as to make an elaborate plan to make a citizen's arrest and have me jailed on the pretext that in praying for the sick I was practicing medicine without a license. Several times these attempts were made but the crowd wouldn't let the men through to me. I had been warned one morning that this night the climax would come. It would be an attempt on my life, or at the least a major effort to stop the meeting on the trumped-up charge. They knew of course in a free society no such charge would hold up in court but failing to stop the meetings any other way, this might embarrass us and hold us up to public ridicule.

All that day I permitted this thing to upset my mind. My body reacted and I couldn't digest my food. Before leaving for the auditorium I did what I always do before attempting to preach and pray for people's healing. I knelt and prayed until the anointing of the Holy Spirit came upon me. This is an intangible move of the Spirit which when it comes upon me is very real to all my senses. I can feel it. It is the living, moving Spirit of God rising irresistibly within me so that I can experience a power from God in which I feel a boldness to face anything!

Early in my ministry I made a twofold vow—to touch neither the gold nor the glory, nor to enter the pulpit without first feeling the anointing of the Holy Spirit, which is the unlimited Christ himself filling me with His holy power from on high.

As I rose, picked up my Bible, and started out the door the Voice spoke, "Expect a miracle. Expect a new miracle every day. Tell your friends and partners to expect a miracle and to expect a new miracle every day."

I remember my flesh tingling as I heard these words. It brought God so close to me.

That night I walked through ten thousand people without a thought of the opposers, the killers, or anything that could stop me. I felt taller because I knew that I knew God had called me to take His healing power to my generation and as long as I obeyed Him I could expect a miracle, a new one every day, including this one tonight. With a new assurance I knew that nothing devised against me would prosper for my trust was in God through whom I could expect a miracle, a new one every day.

Standing before that audience I related this experience. I told of the threats and the presence of the news media to capture it if it happened. I told of something else—the unlimited hope we had if we expected miracles, that as we expected miracles *they would happen*. Each day would bring its new miracles for us. I tell you it was an exciting evening and everything changed for the better.

We heard no more of the intimidating threats. The press was kind enough to carry the news to their readers and the crowds grew larger and even more responsive. Many more conversions and healings happened throughout the remainder of the crusade. In the long run, however, the most important happening was God's revelation to my aching spirit that I could expect a miracle, a new one every day—and that the same commitment from God was to others as well as to myself.

Today, some fifteen years later, I have mailed our little "EXPECT A MIRACLE" plaques to hundreds of thousands. Homes and offices all over the world display them. "Expect a miracle" has become the theme, the rallying point, of this ministry. It has become the hope of millions.

I have received letters—and do daily—from people in virtually every level of life, with about every kind of illness or other problem, who have told me how

EXPECT A MIRACLE gave them a new perspective, a handle for what little faith they had left. They have told me how their lives have been changed by the power of God. Actually they have gotten into *miracle-living* which is what is happening in my life and what I think God wants each of us to have—*every day.*

WHAT GOD SAID TO ME CONCERNING MIRACLES AND THE SCHOOL OF MEDICINE AT ORU

Another word the Lord has given me on these three powerful words, Expect A Miracle, is really tremendous. It, too, came in a time of challenge in my life. God had called me to build Him a School of Medicine and add it to ORU. I know ORU is a miracle in itself. Just walking across the grounds, seeing the faculty and students, I, and almost everyone who visits the University, feel a sense of the miraculous! It's almost like you are on holy ground because it is God's.

While I was trying to bring my mind to focus on the possibility of being able to build God a medical school and finding I could not logically reason it out, God spoke to my spirit:

"Miracles are coming toward you or past you every day."

My first thought was very positive: Lord, if miracles are coming toward me or past me every day, then I'm going to reach out and take mine; I'm not going to let them pass me by.

My thoughts are still positive on: MIRACLES ARE COMING TOWARD YOU OR PAST YOU EVERY DAY. A great many others have exuberantly seized this powerful truth and are receiving miracles they never before had thought possible. I know of no better way to wake up in the morning than by remembering: *Today a miracle is coming toward me and I can receive it.*

HOW THESE THREE MOST POWERFUL WORDS, "EXPECT A MIRACLE," CAN CHANGE YOUR LIFE

Of the many letters people write me, some get hold of me until I am touched in every fiber of my being. I get a lift, or I get a new understanding, or they remind me of something I have said or done and it becomes more meaningful to me.

This letter I am about to share with you will turn you every way but loose. It's from a man here in Oklahoma who needed a miracle desperately, who was so far from it, YET GOT IT.

Can you imagine being on the FBI rap sheet showing 375 arrests on public drunkenness alone? of being kicked out of the navy? so hopeless and helpless that he's absolutely reached the bitter end? Can you imagine all that?

I want him to tell you what three words did for his life . . . then I want you to start looking on your sickness or problem (which is any dis-harmony or dis-ease you have) as something you want to be well *from* . . .

Dear Brother Roberts:

I would like to take this opportunity to tell you how "three words" changed my life. It has been over four years since

I wrote to you. I don't know if you still
have my old letter or not. I wrote it
sitting at the kitchen table, just as
I'm doing now. But today as I write
you, "it's a whole new ball game!"
Brother Roberts, I do hope you will
have time to read this, because I
want you to know about this *miracle*
that God performed through you and A.A.

When I wrote to you four years ago, I
felt so hopeless and helpless, and so
despondent and remorseful that I didn't
know which way to turn. For 33 years of
my life I had tried everything (including the church)! and all to no avail. I
was a helpless and hopeless alcoholic of
the type you would have to know personally
to believe!

Having been born and raised in the Cookson
Hills of Oklahoma, I had early access to
moonshine (white lightning), and at the
early age of 14 I was arrested for public
drunkenness and that was the beginning of
33 years of drunkenness. I was a slave to
the cunning, baffling, and powerful disease
of alcoholism. They kicked me out of the
Navy when I was 19 because I was an alcoholic
and had no willpower against the compulsion
to drink. I went on to be in the gutter
of about every skidrow in the United States
and Mexico. I was hospitalized some 27 times
for alcoholism and have an FBI rap sheet

of 375 arrests for public drunkenness
and I drank everything from paint thinner
to aftershave lotion. Because I was sick,
physically, mentally, and spiritually, ever-
body (including myself) thought me a hopeless case. As I stated earlier in this
letter, you would have had to know
me personally to believe the type of
alcoholic I really was.
Brother Roberts, it's almost too much for
anyone to believe (except God) that a life
such as I have just described to you could
be completely changed by "three words" but
thank God, *it's true*!

I will never forget that day, April 1st, when
I sat at the kitchen table. I had told my
dear wife, I said, "Honey, you know and I
know that I have wasted my life and I'm
hopeless. I was born to die a drunk and
you will be better off when I'm gone." I
was so remorseful and sick in my soul. But
thank God, I went on to say to my wife, "As
a last resort, I'm going to write to Oral
Roberts because I have been inspired by
hearing him talk." And I'm so thankful
that I did write to you.

You answered my letter and in so doing
you and God answered my prayer. You
simply said, *"Expect a Miracle."* And I
believed this! At that time I had nothing else to hang on to, so I hung on to
those three words, until I believed it in

my heart! I kept saying to myself, *"Expect A Miracle!* God has promised it, Oral Roberts has promised it, who am I to say it cannot happen?"* Then, *I did believe it!!* And thank God, it happened!! The miracle had finally happened after 33 years of despair and hell on earth.

Brother Roberts, that has been over four years now and I have not had the desire or compulsion for alcohol since that day when you told me to *"Expect A Miracle!"* I was lifted from the pits of hell on earth, a slave to alcohol, to a happy and normal way of life such as I had never known before. I now have a feeling of usefulness. I'm not hopeless or help-less anymore. I have been reinstated in the Navy and now have an honorable dis-charge. I am now an employee at the very hospital where I was once a patient (seven different times) for alcoholism. The list could go on and on, of the many "miracles" that God has bestowed on me over the past four years.

Brother Roberts, I hope some day that I will have the opportunity to meet you in person and shake your hand and tell you how grateful I'll always be to you and to God for those *three words* you wrote to me that saved my life and let me live a life that I never knew existed.

And now you know why I said, *"It's a whole new ball game."*

At the state hospital where I'm employed, I have the opportunity to help other suffering alcoholics and the first thing I tell them is, "If you are sick like I was and want to get well, *Expect A Miracle!"*

God bless you!

Yours truly,

Floyd Mears

Many things stand out in this letter but to me the best is:

"If you are sick like I was, and want to get well, EXPECT A MIRACLE."

Oh, sure, you can say, "Why that old drunk, he hit bottom and had no way to go but up. What's that got to do with me, I'm not like that?"

True, but don't miss what he's saying. He is saying, "If you are *sick* . . . as I was," not necessarily the sickness he had (though if you are, he includes you), but sick . . . sick because you got hit by something that won't turn you loose— it's anything from alcohol to bitterness to hate to physical illness to fear to loneliness and just plain unwillingness to use your will in the right way.

" . . . and want to get well . . ."

Your WANT TO is a precious power you possess and it's there to work for you. It's that much of God in you, who is for your better health, who wants you to enter into miracle-living. "If you want to get well," think of this possibility that you can, that you will, and you, too, will be saying to someone, "If you are sick like I was, and want to get well, EXPECT A MIRACLE."

Yes, you'll be saying that. I feel it. It will be a whole new ball game, like Floyd Mears said, and you'll again have the chance you wanted. You will have committed to a new possibility in your life . . .

GREAT SELF-STARTERS ABOUT SEED-PLANTING AND EXPECTING A MIRACLE

1. My miracles follow my seed-planting.

2. God is the Source of multiplying my seed sown.

3. I can expect a miracle even when I am about to panic.

4. Miracles are coming toward me or past me every day and I am going to reach out and take mine.

5. Every morning I will face my new day *EXPECTING A MIRACLE!*

 key issue: *Even When It Scares Me I Will Plant Good Seed By Reaching Out To Others*

Chapter 6

HOW I LEARNED TO PLANT GOOD SEED THROUGH OBEDIENCE TO GOD WHEN HE TOLD ME TO TAKE HIS HEALING POWER TO THE PEOPLE

 key issue: **Reaching Out To Others Is Miracle Seed I Am Planting For My Own Healing And Success**

I have known so many people who want a miracle, anything that will get them out of the situation they are in so they can live, LIVE, LIVE. Part of their trouble is, they have living in their mind—not what it takes to make it possible. They have knowingly or unknowingly worked themselves into the jam of wanting something for nothing.

Frankly, I have never received anything for nothing but that later I wished I hadn't. It's the same with everybody I know. It won't work. It's grasping at a straw, and when you get it you discover it won't hold you up.

To rid yourself of any part of wanting something for nothing, accept the fact that God has so constituted you and His world that there is built into you and me the eternal principle of *sowing and reaping*. In the Bible it's called seedtime and harvest.

"While the earth remaineth," God said of the new world after the Flood had destroyed the old one, "seedtime and harvest...shall not cease" (Genesis 8:22).

He says you must sow seed or have a seedtime in order to produce a harvest. You must sow first before you can expect to reap. Your miracle follows your seed-planting.

DO YOU REALIZE YOU HAVE ALREADY SOWN MANY SEEDS?

The fact is that you have sown seed, many seeds. How can you know that? Well, every time you have initiated any positive action for good, you have planted a seed. A smile, a pat on the back, helping somebody, saying a prayer in someone's behalf, giving a gift of your time to a good cause, or money, or a good thought — that is sowing a seed of faith whether you know it or not. That is the seedtime that God referred to in Genesis 8:22. This is what I want you to see that you have done, that it is a seed you have planted; therefore, each of those seeds has a harvest on the end of it. It has a "due season" for you to reap (Galatians 6:9). It took me a long time to start learning this. Since I started, I have come into Seed-Faith living which is the basis for those powerful three words, EXPECT A MIRACLE.

DO YOU ALSO REALIZE IT IS GOD WHO IS THE SOURCE OF MULTIPLYING YOUR SEED SOWN?

Often we say, "I helped this person, now when I need help, why won't he help me?"

True, you have helped him, you planted the seed. BUT you cannot expect the one you helped to be a SOURCE back to you. God is your Source. *No person* has the power to multiply a seed. God alone multiplies your seed sown. God said, "Cast thy bread upon the waters: for thou shalt find it after many days" (Ecclesiastes 11:1). *The wave you cast your bread upon may not be the one upon which it returns. It may be a new wave. Whichever wave it returns on, it will be God who sends it back. He is your Source.* This means the ones you help may or may not help you, but God who is GOD OF THE HARVEST will cause someone to help you. If you keep your trust in Him, He will never, never fail you in this. Like me, you've got to believe this and I do believe it.

Do your best to understand that the seeds you plant to help people are a demonstration of your inner self being on God's side. Further, it is an expression of your deep, deep feelings to do good. It is said of Jesus that He "went about doing good" (Acts 10:38). It is also written that Jesus said, "[I came not] to destroy men's lives, but to save them" (Luke 9:56). He is called in the Bible, "the seed of David" (Romans 1:3; 2 Timothy 2:8).

Like us, He himself is a seed; like us, what He did was a seed He planted. Every thought, every act, every wish, everything He did became an expression of His inner self to heal, to save, to give life and to give it more abundantly. That was the seed He planted.

"BE LIKE JESUS..."

I vividly remember when the Voice said to me, "Be like Jesus and heal the people as He did." I did not understand this at first; it took months, years, before it dawned on me that BEING LIKE JESUS and healing people as He did, is what God is. It is what God's method is. It is the seeds He wants us to plant so He can multiply them back to us to solve our own problems and meet our own needs. Also to open up healing for our own illnesses and bring constant *replenishment* for our daily existence while on earth. You see this, don't you?

God was actually telling me to get into seedtime and harvest, or what I have come to know from Jesus as Seed-Faith (Matthew 17:20).

Not once can you ever find Jesus expecting people to help Him first. He said, "[I] came not to be ministered unto, but . . . to give" (Matthew 20:28). Then to you and me He said, "Give, and it shall be given unto you" (Luke 6:38). Even in the Golden Rule He gave us, "Do unto others as you would have men do unto you" (Luke 6:31), is an action that you *initiate* in your spirit. It is something you DO *first*. "DO" is the first part of the Golden Rule. It is a seed *you* start planting, not the other person. Jesus had our good in mind when in the Golden Rule He told us to start it by DOING something first.

Doing unto others as you would have them do to you is an act of Seed-Faith. It takes faith — and love — to plant a seed like that. We, of course, want others to do nice things to us and for us. However, Jesus says this begins with doing it first to other people. Doing it guarantees that God will cause it to come back to us MULTIPLIED, whether from those we've done it to, or from those we least expect it from. It will come back to us from whatever person or means God chooses to use! He is the Source of its being multiplied back to us!

In Luke 6:38, Jesus says, "For with the same measure ye [give] it shall be [given] to you again." I have found this to be literally true, except it is always MORE than I gave. Because what I give is a seed I plant and when God multiplies the seed it is much more.

In one of our seminars a partner said, "You can count the seeds in an apple but who can count the apples in one seed?"

In one of the question-and-answer periods, another partner said, "God doesn't need our seed, we need His crop." I agree in part. God doesn't need our seed like we need His crop. But He does have to have something from us in order to multiply it back. As I've said before, zero multiplied back equals zero.

THE CAT-SELLER

I heard of a certain man who dealt in antiques. Many of his bargains were obtained from people who didn't know the value of the object this man wanted. One day he came into a secondhand store and saw a cat in the middle of the floor drinking milk from an old bowl. His experienced eye saw immediately that it was no ordinary bowl, it was an antique worth a lot of money. He said to himself, *this fellow doesn't know that's an expensive antique. Why, I can buy it for little or nothing.*

He said to the storekeeper, "Say, I noticed that beautiful cat. I've been looking for a cat like that. I'd like to buy that cat if you're willing to sell it."

The man replied, "Mister, I'll sell anything in my store. You give me $25 and that cat is yours."

He paid him, picked up the cat and began to stroke it. "My, what a beautiful cat," he said. "I've always wanted a cat like this."

Looking down at the bowl, he picked it up and said, "By the way, I notice the cat was drinking milk from this old bowl. It's not worth anything, he's used to it, I believe I'll just take this old bowl with me."

The storekeeper answered, "Mister, you put that bowl down. That's the best cat-seller I've ever had."

What is Seed-Faith or the Golden Rule here? Is it trying to deceive the storekeeper who in turn deceives back? Didn't both men plant a *bad* seed that would be multiplied back in *bad* things? How much better to have taken Jesus' way of giving, and giving first, by one selling for a fair price so the other could receive a fair return? Are we really like the cat-seller? Or do we see that God has something better for us?

AFTER 33 YEARS HE STARTED SOWING GOOD SEED

I discovered later something about my friend, Floyd Mears.

When all the bad seeds he had planted for 33 years brought him a harvest so bad it was totally destroying him as a man, he began to listen to my sermons on television on Seed-Faith. He had been a "taker," with no regard for the jobs he had. He cared nothing for the Navy who took a chance and accepted him. The wife who had loved him—he constantly neglected. The children who were counting on his being a good father—he neglected because his wants were only for himself. He wanted something for nothing.

The deceitful promises of alcohol lay in ashes at the feet of Floyd Mears who in his own way had been the cat-seller and cat-buyer.

He became a sick man. It was at the point of his need that he found God was waiting. The instincts God awakened in him were to listen and start in on the eternal principles of Seed-Faith, of giving — and giving first. This is when he started giving. This was the response my letter struck in him when I wrote, *Expect a Miracle*. He could expect as he now had a basis for expectancy because he had started giving.

You and I must know that anything we get by being a getter instead of a giver will eventually "get" us. It will rise up and bite us. On the other hand, we must know every good seed we plant will, without fail, bring a good harvest.

"Be not deceived, God is not mocked. Whatsoever a man soweth, that shall he also reap" (Galatians 6:7). Best of all, God says that seedtime is followed by harvesttime.

A TEST OR A REWARD

Everything in life is either a TEST OR A REWARD. At least, it is a *test* of your response to life, by your spirit, your better self, OR it is a *reward* coming back as a harvest for the good seed you have planted.

A rejected opportunity to give is a lost opportunity to receive. Jesus said that in these words: "It is more blessed to give than to receive" (Acts 20:35). The word *blessed,* as used by Jesus here, means *productive.* Jesus is saying it is more productive to give than to receive. Why is giving more productive?

Because only what you give can be multiplied back, not what you receive.

Remember, in God's eternal law of seedtime and harvest, IF YOU GIVE NOTHING AND NOTHING IS MULTIPLIED, IT IS STILL NOTHING! Zero multiplied by zero remains zero! This really inspires me to give. When you see the good that is sure to come back, it brings you into joy. You become cheerful in your giving. Expecting a miracle—or the harvest—becomes God's commitment to you. Then you don't have to blunder through life by expecting something for nothing. You will know the rewards of working, giving, expecting, AND RECEIVING.

THINGS I NEED TO REMEMBER ABOUT SEED-PLANTING:

1. **There is no such thing as "something for nothing."**

2. **Seed planting produces a harvest—it is God's eternal law of sowing and reaping (Genesis 8:22).**

3. **It is God who multiplies the seed sown.**

4. **Everything in life is either a test or a reward.**

5. **A rejected opportunity to give is a lost opportunity to receive.**

6. I do not have to blunder through life expecting something for nothing when I can know the rewards of working, giving, expecting, and receiving.

 key issue:

Reaching Out To Others Is
Miracle Seed I Am Planting
For My Own Healing
And Success

A SUMMARY OF STEP NUMBER TWO...

Things I must do and remember as I plant the good seed of loving God and reaching out to people:

key issue:

1. **I WILL LOOK TO GOD ALONE AS MY SOURCE AND NOT TO PEOPLE.** *If I think I don't like God, I will tell Him how I feel and then plant a Seed-Faith prayer for one I don't like and it will be multiplied back to me at the point of my need.*

key issue:

2. **I WILL PRAY FOR PEOPLE I LIKE OR DISLIKE BECAUSE GOD LOVES THEM ALL.** *I can overcome the things I don't like about God when I get this truth inside me: God is my Source.*

key issue:

3. **PRAYING FOR SOMEONE ELSE WILL BEGIN A MIRACLE IN ME.** *The way to miracle-living is: giving God my best and then*

asking Him for His best...a miracle...and expecting it so that I will receive it as His good for my life and my loved ones.

key issue: 4. **I WILL LIVE MY LIFE RIGHT EVERY DAY THROUGH GOD MY SOURCE AND MY STRENGTH.** *If I feel I have lost my way, I will get honest with God and man and I will look to God, my Source, who restores me.*

key issue: 5. **EVEN WHEN IT SCARES ME I WILL PLANT GOOD SEED BY REACHING OUT TO OTHERS.** *Miracles are coming toward me or past me. I will face every new day looking to God as the multiplier of my seed sown, and expecting a miracle.*

key issue: 6. **REACHING OUT TO OTHERS IS MIRACLE SEED I AM PLANTING FOR MY OWN HEALING AND SUCCESS.** *Seed-planting produces a harvest— it is God's eternal law of sowing and reaping (Genesis 8:22).*

Step Number

THREE

You can expect many miracles
for yourself if you have a right
relationship with yourself . . .
and with God.

Chapter 1

HOW TO LOVE YOURSELF AS GOD LOVES YOU SO YOU CAN LIVE IN A STATE OF BETTER HEALTH AND SUCCESS

 key issue: **I Am Using My Inborn Ability To Believe And Exercising My Faith To Get Well And Stay Well**

For many years after having dealt with people throughout the world, both in person and through correspondence, I have felt they should have better health and live longer than is ordinarily expected.

Imagine my surprise—and joy—when I began running into mounting medical evidence gained from in-depth research that our bodies should respond better and be in better health a much longer time on earth.

The researchers have learned, for example, that the body's organs don't deteriorate dramatically with age. The healthy heart doesn't age significantly, they say. They indicate the loss of brain cells in old age is not universal. Healthy organs in our mature years tell us we have a greater expectancy for health and longer life.

In 1900, life expectancy in this country for men was about 46 years and for women about 48. Today, it is 69 and 76 respectively.

I read in one medical journal where it stated they are talking now of the probability of extending healthy life far beyond what we know it today. It is even stated that if a person at his healthiest can be handled right, his life-span can be extended up to 200, 300, or even 400 years. Incredible? Yes.

My prayer is that the researchers will learn more and more and pass it on to us SO WE CAN PUT IT INTO OUR RESPONSE TO LIFE. Believing it helps it increase health in you.

Am I saying that this kind of healing is related to faith in God?

Yes, I am.

St. Paul says God has given to every person the measure of faith (Romans 12:3). Your innate ability to believe, to exercise this inborn faith, is your strongest power to get well, stay well, stay alive longer! It's all a part of God who wants to be as much a part of you as your breathing—and as close!

THE EXPERIENCE OF A YOUNG 92-YEAR-OLD CAN ADD HEALTH AND YEARS TO YOUR LIFE

I remember praying for a 92-year-old man in one of our crusades who was still quite vigorous. As he stood before me, I asked, "What is your particular need?"

"Oh," he replied, "I want to make it to a hundred."

"Do you think you can?"

"Oh, yes, with just a little touch of God's healing power."

He looked straight at me as if I might not respond. He said, "Young man, why not? Why not go on to 100?"

I said, "I'm not against it," and smiled.

He said, "I have able doctors and I cooperate with what they tell me to do. I take long walks and keep myself in shape. I control the amount of food I eat. I don't abuse my body or my mind. And I am a Christian!"

"How long have you been a Christian?" I asked.

"Many years. I believe God wants me to have health. That's why I listen to my doctors. And it's why I listen to you. That's why I'm here. Just being in this atmosphere of faith lifts my spirit. Already, I feel better, stronger, more alive. If you will say a prayer for me, I believe I can make it to a hundred."

The entire crusade audience applauded.

I asked him what his loved ones thought about this.

He must have thought I was referring to someone's opposition to my prayers for the healing of people. He bristled a moment and said, "Son, if they say anything about Oral Roberts or about God not being able to heal folks, well, I just mark 'em off my list."

Again the crowd roared. But he was serious. He believed God wanted him to have health, to make it to a hundred.

I prayed for him; he hugged me and walked off as if he owned the world.

YOU HAVE A LOT MORE GOING FOR YOU TODAY

But there's more, much more to this man's goal and spirit than we may think. Medicine is better, people are exercising and watching their weight better, knowledge of proper diet is better, expectancy for a long life is better, more people believe in healing prayer, there's more positiveness in many people toward God, in being able to use their faith as never before. Millions are catching on to the miracle of Seed-Faith* and its three miracle keys:

(1) Making God the Source of my total supply.
(2) Giving and giving first, giving not as a debt I owe but as a seed I sow.
(3) Expecting a miracle or a harvest from each seed planted coming back in the form of my need.

A human being has a lot more going for him today. I often feel stronger and better now than I did in my thirties. So does Evelyn, my darling wife.

I notice here at Oral Roberts University that the general health of those on our staff and faculty and in our student body is on an astonishingly high level. Of course there is an atmosphere of positive faith in God on the ORU campus that contributes to better health and miracle-living. The Prayer Tower at its center radiates God's healing love. The chapel services twice weekly are filled with God's Word, songs of love and faith, fellowship—deep and spiritual—and a zest for living the abundant life. And, we have splendid medical care.

On these 500 acres there seems to be the feeling from almost every faculty and staff member, every student, "I wish for you the abundant life of our Lord Jesus Christ." Believe me, that's important.

Many people visiting our campus have said they feel this the moment they drive through the Avenue of Flags entrance to the campus.

---

*See back page of this book on how to get my two books on Seed-Faith, free and postpaid.

A HEALING WHILE DRIVING ONTO THE ORU CAMPUS

One man told us, "We were driving west and when we reached Tulsa we decided to drive through the campus. I had been suffering with cancer and was on my way to a specialist in a large city. Well, when we drove into the entrance, I noticed the flags of the nations representing the student body. Then I looked up and saw the Prayer Tower and I felt faith leap in my heart. I felt health start to flow into me. I guess it was an expectancy for a miracle I had gained from reading your book, *A Daily Guide To Miracles*. Anyway, before we finished touring the campus we met students who smiled, spoke to us, or waved at us. There was something there, I knew it. I felt it.

"Getting back into the car to leave, I said to my wife, 'Honey, something warm is going through me.'

"She said, 'What is it?'

"I said, 'It's God. I'm being healed.'

"All the way to the clinic I grew stronger. Later I was dismissed from the clinic on the basis that apparently I had had a wrong diagnosis. Of course they had my records and knew something unusual had happened to me. I knew it too. The draining away of my life, the pain, the loss of weight, began to leave. I am well."

He added, "All I can say is, I feel I ran into an atmosphere of health which I felt surrounding me, infilling me, and restoring me."

I can't explain all this, neither can my staff. Whatever it was eating away at his life left him, and I appreciate it. We see this happen often.

Follow me as closely as you can now for I am going to tell you . . .

HOW YOU CAN LOVE YOURSELF AS GOD LOVES YOU SO YOU CAN EXPECT BETTER HEALTH AND SUCCESS

1. Now say to yourself the key issue: I am using my inborn ability to believe, and exercising my faith to get well and stay well.

2. I will listen to my doctor and believe God wants me to have health.

3. There is more going for me in the way of medicine, exercise, diet, and prayer —all instruments to help me live in a state of better health and success.

4. Being in an atmosphere of faith helps me.

key issue:

I Am Using My Inborn Ability To Believe And Exercising My Faith To Get Well And Stay Well

Chapter 2

HOW TO AVOID WRONG BELIEVING THAT KEEPS YOU FROM BETTER HEALTH AND SUCCESS

 key issue: **I Value Every Instrument Of Healing, And Love The Source Of It All — God**

I want you to get a right theology of healing. Now don't get scared of the word *theology.* Whether you know it or not, everybody has a theology. If you have a good theology you have a firm base upon which to believe in God's healing power. If you have a bad theology, then you don't have much of a foundation to believe anything good about God. And this is where a lot of people are, they are so negative they don't believe much of anything. They have a bad theology about health and miracle-living; therefore, they are missing out on the abundant life that Jesus has promised (John 10:10).

WHAT IS A GOOD THEOLOGY OF HEALING?

What is a good theology of healing? First, it is based upon the life of God himself as He has dealt with man from the very beginning. From the beginning of time it has been God's highest wish, will, and purpose to give people *life*. Therefore, it is important that you *take time* in reading the Bible. This is very important to you for your well-being. Start with Genesis, the first book, and read the Bible through. Take the time to do it—you will be glad you did. As you read your Bible, observe *the key issue*—which is the way God looks at man, the good that God wants man to have, and the good that He wants man to be. And remember that God is the key issue of the Bible.

ESPECIALLY STUDY THE FOUR GOSPELS AND THE BOOK OF ACTS IN THE NEW TESTAMENT

Study the Four Gospels—St. Matthew, St. Mark, St. Luke, and St. John—and the book of Acts. These first five books in the New Testament clearly concentrate upon the life and ministry of Jesus. (They are the only ones in the entire Bible that do.) As I studied these books I saw Jesus as a man of power, compassion, and action. He walked and talked with all kinds of people. He wanted men to live freely and fully. Jesus learned the importance of responding to life with His spirit first. He showed that God loves people, and demonstrated it by forgiving sins, by healing the sick, and by meeting people's needs in every level of their lives. In doing these things He showed us what God is like. You see Jesus at work and it is God at work. He showed us that God is more than an idea, or concept. He is our Creator, our Redeemer and Savior, our Source, our life itself in true fullness and livability.

THIS IS OUR GOD

Did you know *Christ never made anybody sick?* *He was against sickness.* In no place will you ever find that Jesus was *for* sickness. He had an attitude against it. This means God doesn't go around giving people cancer or other dread diseases. God doesn't go around seeking to hurt people. Everything that is good is from God. Every bad thing is from the devil (John 10:10). *One reason I respect doctors so much is that they have grasped this eternal truth and are against sickness and FOR HEALTH.* Consciously or unconsciously they have a pretty good theology of healing. Sometimes I wish we who are preachers had such a good theology of healing. If all of us had a better theology of healing we would be less inclined to argue about whether it's God's *will* to heal or not. We would positively approach people with hurts and ills with Christ's own attitude of wholeness for them. I speak out of experience when I say this. For I know HEALING BEGINS IN THIS LIFE. You have this wonderful claim upon the very real promise of God which is intended personally for you and your loved ones in the NOW.

DO YOU KNOW IT'S GOD'S NATURE TO HEAL?

As you study Jesus you will see that His healing ministry began in the very nature of God that runs like a single thread through the Bible. The healing power of Jesus flowed out of Him because He was full of it. The woman that touched the hem of His garment (she was hemorrhaging to death) felt His healing power restoring her to wholeness, and He said

He felt the healing go out of Him (Mark 5:25-30). So when you look at Jesus you look at someone who is full of God's healing power; and in *any way you can touch Him, His healing power is going to flow directly toward you for the purpose of making you whole.* Remember, Jesus' healing power flows out of Him for you to receive into your own self. Reach out and touch Him.

DELIVERY SYSTEMS OF HEALTH FOR YOU

Every skill that any human has, including that of a minister, a doctor, a businessman, a farmer, a laborer, a housewife—any honest skill—is a God-given skill. We have to work and cultivate God-given talents and skills, but all good comes from God (James 1:17). And there is a coming together for the first time, at least in my lifetime, of the different delivery systems of God's healing power. To me, ALL HEALING IS DIVINE whether it seems to be secular or seems to be spiritual. God simply uses DIFFERENT DELIVERY SYSTEMS to bring better health and miracle-living to us.

As I said, I appreciate the fact that the medical profession is against disease and for health and well-being. I just wish all of us in the ministry of the gospel had the same hatred for disease and that same great belief in health and well-being that doctors have. I wish we would acknowledge that God does heal. It is His nature to heal. In addition, He has put a built-in system of healing in us.

I am grateful that today we are seeing great changes in the attitude of both religion and medicine toward healing. We are seeing a great many doctors who are practicing at the top level of their competence who also believe that *the inner spirit of man* has to be touched by a Greater Power . . . and can be! Also, we are seeing preachers and priests and lay people of the church believing in both medicine and prayer for healing. They gladly accept the great God-given compassion and hard-worked-for skill that the physician brings. They also appreciate the vast healing power of prayer. I see these two delivery systems — prayer and medicine — coming together more and more every day, and people are in position to benefit more as they open themselves up to whatever delivery system God can use to cure or restore them. God wants you well!

It was 1974 and I was standing on the platform of the Mabee Center here at Oral Roberts University. It was the closing day of a seminar for Christian lay people. There were about 2,000 in attendance and it was time for the healing service. The people were coming for the laying on of hands as a point of contact to release their faith. And some of the medical doctors in Tulsa, who are my close friends and who are also Spirit-filled, were helping me with healing prayers that day. And right in the midst of all this the Lord spoke to my heart and said, "They that are sick need a physician" (Luke 5:31).

Well, I knew that was in the Bible. But the Lord just kept impressing me with those words until I said, "Lord, what are You trying to say to Me?"

And He said, "When I was here in My humanity I used both prayer and physicians — remember St. Luke, the physician . . ."

So I began to reread the Gospel of St. Luke and

the book of The Acts of the Apostles which St. Luke
wrote. And I began to better understand the relationship of Jesus and doctors, and to see how both natural
and supernatural healing powers are to work together
for the healing of people, thus demonstrating that
ALL HEALING IS DIVINE. I had known this for
many years but now it seemed to come into proper
focus for me in the ministry of healing.

JESUS SAID THE SICK
NEED A DOCTOR

Doctor Luke records Jesus as saying, *"They that
are whole need not a physician; but they that are
sick"* (Luke 5:31). So we have Jesus healing not only
by faith but also by putting within that sphere of
healing the physician, which means from our Lord's
standpoint, ALL HEALING IS DIVINE whether it's
medical or by prayer and faith.

As you read in the book of Acts and in Colossians
4:14, you will find that a medical doctor was a
member of the official evangelistic team of St. Paul.
This medical doctor's name was Luke. He joined
St. Paul's healing ministry and traveled with him in
the capacity of a physician and ministered God's
divine healing with Paul. They also worked together
establishing churches throughout the then-known
world. Luke later wrote the Gospel of Luke and The
Acts of the Apostles in the New Testament. Also,
St. Luke is the one who said more about the actual
working of miracles of healing by the Holy Spirit than
any other New Testament writer, for along with St. Paul
he was very much in the move of the Holy Spirit
in that day.

Probably because St. Luke was a medical doctor, he tells more of the human or domestic side of Jesus. He, no doubt, spent many hours with Mary, the mother of Jesus, and tells about the life of her Son from Mary's viewpoint. It is obvious that he talked to her. He listened to her. And he was able to record little-known incidents about the babyhood and childhood of Jesus. He is the only one who relates the story of the Child Jesus as He grew: "And Jesus increased in wisdom and stature, and in favor with God and man" (Luke 2:52). He told how Jesus was left in the temple when He was only 12 years old and how Mary and Joseph had to retrace their steps to find Him. They found Him where they had left Him—among the doctors of law in the temple, answering their questions. And the lawyers were amazed at the wisdom of this Child Jesus (Luke 2:42-48).

St. Luke, as a physician, was interested in the human side of Jesus' life, the domestic side of life, *because he knew this was the level on which people have to live every day.* It's like the woman who said, "The trouble with life is it's so *daily.*"

Life *is* daily and thank God, He is "daily" too. He helps us understand how to use whatever way He has provided on this earth to receive our healing and to live in health in our total being.

HEALING THROUGH SURGERY

I'm reminded of one of my dear partners, an insurance man, who lost the sight in his right eye due to a blow on the head. The retina was detached and in addition to the loss of sight he couldn't stoop or bend over or do anything like this because the pain would become so excruciating. As a result, he had a life of inactivity for about six months. Then his doctor referred him to a specialist. When the specialist examined my friend, he saw that he was hemorrhaging in that eye and put him in surgery immediately. He said, "You know and I know that I'm not God, but I believe I can help you." So this young doctor operated and with his God-given skill put the retina back in place. In about six months my friend was seeing in that eye again. *God used the skill of a surgeon and modern technology to bring healing to my friend's eye.* So I thank God for His delivery system of medical skill, and at the same time I hold Him in loving awe for His ability to heal through the prayer of faith which I continually witness daily.

I recently witnessed a man's blind eyes opening right in front of me. After receiving prayer he very quietly said, "Thank You, God. I can see. I knew it would happen." This was without an operation—a miracle, really. But is it any greater miracle than the sight my friend received through surgery? Somehow we've got to close the gap between healing by medicine and healing by prayer. More and more I am seeing it is usually a combination of both. All healing comes from God and I am comfortable in accepting and being a part of it. In fact, I am aggressive about it.

A SCHOOL OF MEDICINE

In 1961, four years before we opened the doors of Oral Roberts University, God spoke to me concerning the students He would send to enroll, "I want you to raise up your students to hear My voice, to go where My voice is heard small, where My light is dim, and My power is not known...to go even to the uttermost bounds of the earth. Their work will exceed yours and in this I am well pleased."

He let me know that after ORU had been opened and well established, I was to build a medical school, a school sending out Spirit-filled physicians, young Lukes who are an extension of God's call to me, who will take His healing power to this generation...and beyond.

The Lord said, "They are going to go with medicine, but you are going to teach them how to share My healing power through prayer too. They are going to be young men and women of prayer as well as well-trained and dedicated physicians. And they are going to go into nations that are now being closed to the type of missionaries who have only a preaching ministry. They are going to go to the uttermost bounds of the earth." Then He added, "When I told you to take My healing power to your generation I meant not only through prayer but medicine, too, for all My healing power is for man."

He showed me that He would use all His healing systems in my ministry—that I was to take His healing, His total healing power, to my generation. Remember this, regardless of the delivery system, God is your SOURCE for healing.

IT IS IMPORTANT FOR YOU TO KNOW GOD IS YOUR SOURCE FOR HEALING

God says, "I am the Lord that healeth thee" (Exodus 15:26).

People say, "The medicine the doctor gave me cured me." Not so. The medicine comes from God's natural resources in and on this earth—such as a plant or an animal; therefore, God is the SOURCE and He heals you through one or more of His delivery systems. It could have been the doctor's skill in using medicine.

People say, "Well, the natural forces of my body went to work and I'm feeling fine now." True. But who created your body with built-in powerful healing forces? God, who is its SOURCE.

People say, "This man or woman prayed for me and healed me." They prayed but they didn't heal you. God, who hears and answers the prayer of faith, did the healing. Prayer and faith are only instruments, or delivery systems; *the SOURCE is God*.

It is very important to you to know the difference between SOURCE and INSTRUMENT.

SOURCE is like a tree; INSTRUMENT is like the fruit produced by the tree. Pay attention to the tree by cultivating it and seeing that it is kept healthy and the fruit will be there in its season. But neglect the source of the fruit and soon it will dry up and cease to produce.

For example, medicine is an instrument.

The natural forces of your body are instruments.

Prayer, as you offer it to God in faith, is an instrument.

A person with faith in God praying for you is an instrument.

Seed-Faith giving is an instrument, a powerful one, for it is a seed you plant from which you expect a miracle.

Other things such as climate, or love and understanding, or counseling, or asking for forgiveness, or apologizing to a person you have wronged—all these are instruments.

THE SOURCE OF THESE INSTRUMENTS IS GOD. God is your Source. You must always look beyond the instrument to the Source.

As a doctor told me, "Oral, I've learned from the Bible, and from hearing you and reading your books, something that makes my practice a real joy and it's this, I *value* the instrument of healing but I *worship* the *Source* of it—God!"

I replied, "Doctor, I've never heard it expressed exactly like that but I believe it 100 percent."

A WORD OF CAUTION

We now know God uses different delivery systems of His healing power such as faith and such as medicine. But a word of caution here is important.

Take faith. *You can have faith in faith rather than faith in God* (its Source and object), *and fail.*

Take medicine. You can put all your hopes in it instead of a divinely given instrument from God, your Source, and also fail.

In fact, we humans are so complex and our understanding of God and His ways of doing things so limited, that sometimes seemingly with the best faith or the best medicine or the best of both we suffer failure.

Of course we must never forget the Bible teaches that each of us is going to die. "It is appointed unto men once to die, after this the judgment" (Hebrews 9:27). Death is a divine appointment. Death is classed as an enemy, our final enemy. But even in the process of dying I have seen miraculous things happen—release from pain, even the disappearance of the disease. You may ask, how then could the person die? Because there is a *time* to die, as well as a time to be born (Ecclesiastes 3:2). Sick or well, you are going to die. Sickness unchecked can hasten it. However, when death's time comes nothing will hold it back. We must be prepared to go at any moment (right in our heart with God and people).

A WORD OF GREAT HOPE

While God is not the source of death, He is the *Source of Life*. Because He is the Source of both abundant life here on earth and eternal life beyond this life, death is only an interruption. Really, it is a transition from the limited stage of the senses to the stage of the unlimited eternal existence God has in store for everyone who is born of His Spirit.

I've often said, "I want to live, to be alive in every fiber of my being. I want to live in health, well-being, and miracle-living. I want to live every moment until I die. But when my death time comes I want to meet my divine appointment without fear, without resentment and bitterness. I want to embrace it and pass through it into the fullness of that eternal life that began in me the moment Christ came into my heart when I was born again. Above all, I want to look beyond death to my RESURRECTION which is both Christ (who said, I am the Resurrection) and a healing and restoring process of my total being after death. The greatest healing of all is in the resurrection."

A good theology for better health and miracle-living—I call it ABUNDANT LIFE—is to put your faith and expectation in God your Source, and to properly value and accept any instrument as just that, an instrument. As my doctor friend says, "Value the instrument but worship the Source who is God."

A good theology for healing is very important to you—through it you will understand God's great desire to give you better health and miracle-living.

THINGS I NEED TO REMEMBER ABOUT WRONG BELIEVING THAT WOULD KEEP ME FROM BETTER HEALTH AND SUCCESS

1. If I have a good theology of healing I have a firm base upon which to believe God for healing.

2. I have a measure of faith (*Romans 12:3*).

3. I know healing begins in this life—my life.

4. I know Jesus, when He was on earth, showed us our need of both the physician and the power of healing prayers.

5. God is the Source of my healing.

6. I value the instrument of healing but I worship the Source of it—God.

7. *Because I make God my Source, I can expect Him to open up the proper instrument through which to work His healing wonders in me.*

 key issue: *I Value Every Instrument Of Healing, And Love The Source Of It All— God*

Chapter 3

WHETHER YOU FEEL GOOD ENOUGH OR NOT YOU CAN STILL HAVE BETTER HEALTH AND SUCCESS

 key issue: **I Know Jesus Recognizes My Humanity And Wants To Heal Me Because I Am An Important Person**

Often I look back upon the major healing I had—from tuberculosis and stuttering—and the many other healings from various afflictions I've had since, both through healing prayers and medical science.

Often I seek to find what I did to help bring the cure. What state of mind was I in? What was my degree of spirituality? What attitude was I in at the time?

Then I compare this with the two most common things that are said to me by people who get ill.

1. Why has this happened to me? What have I done to deserve it? What kind of God is it who will let this happen to me or my loved ones?

2. Am I good enough to ask God to heal me? Am I worthy?

These things run through my mind occasionally, and from what I hear I know they run through other people's minds. But through the years the Lord has given me some concepts about the humanity of Jesus that have helped me reach an understanding that has been an enormous help to me. And I have testimonies from thousands of others who say it has helped them too. Perhaps this will help you at a direct point of need in your life.

FIRST, THE POSITION IN LIFE
YOU HOLD

As far as I can determine by reading Jesus' life and ministry, He seemed to be in a continuous position of health being constantly self-renewed in His being.

He was involved with the total environment —
the weather,
the mountains and valleys,
the swamps,
the towns and cities,
the favor and disfavor of the people,
the negative attitudes of certain religious leaders,
the relationships with His brothers and sisters
who brought both joy and problems into His life,
with His mother who seemed to both understand
and misunderstand His mission; threats and acts
of assassination against Him, intrigues He had to
face, His own humanity that often rebelled against
the sufferings He had to undergo to take man's
place, the constant learning process He passed
through to know His human self, the agony of
facing the cross when His sweat became as blood
— and probably most serious of all, throwing himself against the devil's opposition of people through
sin, disease, demons, fear, and lack in their lives.

In that position in life one can look at Jesus and see His humanness, especially in the Garden of Gethsemane when his humanness pleaded with God to take the cup of suffering—the cross—away but submitting to it by making His will God's will.

Finally, Jesus, who was able to save and heal others, heard men taunt Him while He was being crucified. "If you are really the Son of God, come down" and, "He saved others; let him save himself" (Luke 23:35). That must have been the cruelest blow of all. But He didn't strike back. He talked with His Father and held on until He could say, "It is finished" (John 19:30) and, "Father, into thy hands I commend my spirit" (Luke 23:46).

Jesus did save and heal others, large numbers of them.

One was a military man maintaining Roman rule over the land of Israel, carrying out Rome's wishes. As an overlord this man besought Christ to heal his servant or aide—and Jesus did it. He did it for a man whose position was a soldier, a captain, part of whose mission included killing people they considered enemies.

In the Old Testament the prophet Elisha brought healing to the general of the Syrian army, who had developed leprosy.

The position of Jesus was one of obedience to God in which His own self-renewal of health seemed to take place. The position of these two military leaders was concerned as much with destroying their enemies as saving other lives.

Were these men good enough? Most of us would say no.

In addition, both men were healed at a distance from Jesus, showing there is NO DISTANCE IN PRAYER.

Your position in life may be perfect, or it may leave

a lot to be desired. I face people in virtually every conceivable position when I pray for their healing. I see the so-called "most committed to God" get healed, and I see some of them fail to get healed. I see some of the "so-called worst" get healed, and some fail to be healed.

I've concluded that in the humanness of Jesus He recognizes our humanness. He seems to want to heal people because they are *people.* Likewise, we in the ministry of healing want to help people because they are people, whether they are good or bad as people see them, or whether they are successful or a failure. I am thankful to God I can help some.

In my own healing from tuberculosis, I had lived a very ungodly and rebellious life. Yet some weeks prior to my healing I repented and gave my life to God. At that time I didn't know I was going to be healed. My sister Jewel had not said those seven wonderful words, "Oral, God is going to heal you." My brother Elmer had not come to carry me to be prayed for. I had seen the image of Christ in my father; it had touched my soul and I wanted Christ to come into my heart and to give me a new birth. I was a saved person when Christ healed my body, but to say I was good enough isn't correct. I had cried, "Why has this happened to me; what have I done to deserve it?" many times, even after my conversion.

In my 30 years of praying for the healing of thousands, I've prayed for the saved and unsaved and I've seen healings of both.

However, in most instances these individuals were getting into a good spiritual relationship with God, or were beginning to recognize God as their Source.

SECOND, WHAT IS YOUR ATTITUDE— YOUR MOTIVATION?

Attitude is about everything. Marriages break up or grow cold because one or both partners develop a bad attitude. Their motivation is not strong. They give in to deadly negative feelings instead of aggressively determining to be positive in their loving responses to each other.

You can get skeptical and destroy your faith so completely that neither prayer, medicine, nor surgery can be of much help. We see this all too often. On the other hand, I'm seeing less and less skepticism and more and more faith. It's really heartening.

Curiosity is different from skepticism. I've seen thousands watch as I prayed for the sick. They were drawn because of honest wonderment. *Can God really heal? Does He heal? I would like to see someone healed.*

But I've usually been able to discern skepticism whenever it is near me, in a large crowd or in an individual. It is so deadly I sense it instantly.

I remember a family bringing their little boy suffering with Perthes' disease. The parents were full of faith as they helped him up on the ramp so I could reach over and pray for the child. Accompanying them were some other members of the family whose spirit reached clear up to where I was sitting and waiting. Had they had a healthy curiosity I would not have done what I did. Their skepticism or hard-core disbelief was so powerful it seemed to freeze the atmosphere of faith in which we had been ministering all evening.

I said to them, "Why don't you folks step off the ramp so we can have a little more room?" With a look of scorn they slowly walked away. The parents were so involved with believing for a miracle they didn't seem to notice. When I prayed for the little boy I asked him if he believed God could make him walk. With a bright face he said, "Yes."

I asked him what he felt like doing. He replied, "Running."

His parents heard this; and quickly unstrapping him from the harness holding one leg off the floor, and taking his crutches, they turned him loose. He hit the floor of the ramp and he started running, leaving the ramp and racing up and down the aisles where the people sat. The people leaped up and there was a roar, a shout of joy from over 10,000 throats.

When the little boy returned to the ramp and I asked the people to sit down, they ignored me. Some were weeping, some were rejoicing out loud, all were deeply moved. So I said, "Well, just help yourselves," and they did.

It took a full ten minutes for things to quiet down so I could question the little boy and have his reply, also to get his parents' comments.

The dad was one of those steady Christians, while his mother was a little more emotionally moved. She had been fasting and praying, she said, for three or four days and believed God would heal her child. The father didn't say much, adding only, "I knew he would get healed."

The little boy was too excited to talk. He stood there, moving from one foot to the other, raising one leg then the other. He really had freedom of movement.

After asking them to return to their physician for a checkup, I let them go.

In the Columbus, Ohio, crusade, one of the largest of my ministry, we had a similar case, about the same age—maybe 12 or 13, and though I prayed the same way (the little boy couldn't walk without his crutches), he slumped to the floor. A wave of fear swept through the audience, and through me too, momentarily. I prayed again, so did the parents, but nothing happened. All I could think of doing was to ask them to bring him the next night and we would pray for him first. They consented and were back with him the following evening. I explained it all to the crowd, many of whom had been there and seen the apparent failure the previous evening. Thank God, our prayers seemed to get through this time and the boy received help, but not as instantaneous as the other little boy had. Nevertheless, this little boy was helped enough to walk without his crutches. Now don't ask me, "What's the difference?" In my humanness, I don't know. But I would like to think that the climate of faith, virtually void of cynicism and criticism and doubt, was present. But in the final analysis, I just don't know. I do know God works in His own will and His own way.

THIRD! WHAT ABOUT THE CONDITION OF THE ONE MINISTERING HEALING?

My humanness sticks out a lot. I get impatient, irritable, stubborn, and sometimes in such a state my darling wife Evelyn has a hard time calming me down. I admit this is a weakness which I've been working to overcome for many years.

Some say I have mellowed but I don't know. I know this, however, God has to work me over from time to time.

I believe my heart is tender, my motivation is good, and my intentions are entirely sincere. A swelled head has never been one of my problems, rather feeling inadequate and unworthy has been more like it in me.

I've noticed when I have a high average of healings, seemingly one right after the other getting healed; I start thinking, why this is not so hard; God is really using me. I've noticed every time, though, that about the time I start feeling this way someone will come before me for healing prayers and I am powerless. Nothing seems to work whether I pray soft or loud, touch or don't touch them, cry or rejoice, nothing works. A failure can plummet me to the depths of despair and I cry, "God, why do You make me so effective with some and I'm such a failure with others?"

I've had few answers on this. It seems a test to see if I will continue.

In the early days I once asked God, "In praying for the sick, what if I fail?" Quickly, in my spirit I heard God say, "You've already done that."

The clear emphasis to me was I had only one way to go and that was UP.

Did Jesus ever fail? Most people think not. Yet at Nazareth where he grew up and He returned to preach and heal, there was an attitude present in which He could not heal (Mark 6:5). He could not.

I take no pleasure from that but I know it by experience. For whatever reason, I know that despite the best efforts of myself, the best efforts of the most successful physicians and surgeons, and even the best cooperation of the sick, there are sometimes seemingly no cures.

Some of my associates through the years have suggested I not be so frank concerning my failures, lest it destroy someone's faith. But I have to live with myself and so far I've not seen the faith of any person seriously seeking God for healing, hurt by my frankness. It seems to me people believe even more in my prayers today than ever before. Perhaps they can sense in all my shortcomings that I am dedicated and honest.

Doctor friends have told me there are days they don't seem to "have it." They say a family squabble can hinder them or they are hindered when they are not feeling well physically themselves. They also say that even under the most desirable conditions there is no sure way of getting the job done as they desire. They say healing science is not a perfect art.

Still, the needs of people are there. Generally I find that we humans who have serious needs are pretty reasonable to deal with. I think there may be some who are mad at themselves and mad at the world. Apparently, there are times when doctors, or persons like myself who have a prayer ministry of healing the sick, and who try to help them, get turned off completely. In such instances we have to go to the next person who really wants help and is ready to take us as we are and hope in God for the best to happen. I know one thing, from a personal standpoint I am a much better instrument for people with this attitude.

A PASTOR AND JESUS

I am deeply moved by the experience of a certain pastor who let his theological knowledge prevent him from preaching practical sermons. His concern to preach great sermons overrode his feelings for the individuals and families in his congregations.

One day he discovered a note on the pulpit. It read, "Dear Pastor, we would see Jesus." He stumbled through his sermon that Sunday morning and afterward slipped away into a quiet room and spent several hours in meditation and soul-searching.

"Could it be," he asked himself, "I've lost Jesus from my heart and from my preaching? Do I no longer really care about people and their needs?"

He had to admit the possibility. Through the following week he kept asking himself, "Do I feel the same compassion for the sick, the fearful, the needy as my Lord did? Is my theological discussions, which I call my sermons, so much directed to the heads of the people that I have forgotten they have hearts and they have troubles and they don't feel Jesus coming through me to them?"

One evening he had it out with himself and Jesus. Falling to his knees he let the tears flow and his heart reach out for the Living Christ and His healing love.

The next several Sundays he preached like a man on fire. His sermons cut through high-sounding phrases and carried straight to the heart and to the needs of the people.

Crowds increased. People were buzzing about their "new" pastor. People began accepting Christ, healings were being reported among the members.

One Sunday when he entered the pulpit, another note was on the podium. It read, "Then were the disciples glad when they saw the Lord."

I know of several churches—one in particular—like that now. You can't get a seat if you don't come early. There's fire and compassion, faith and feeling, love and concern from the pulpit. People, wrestling in the cold of their terrible needs and problems, are overflowing that large church to feel the warmth of the Living Christ. The Holy Spirit is working His miracles and the people are excited.

At some other places I know where the gospel is supposed to be preached, there is a dullness and listlessness in pulpit and pew. Nothing of a vital spiritual and healing nature is happening. The disappointment is so strong you can feel it.

BUT IT'S STILL HAPPENING

I notice whenever the church services are not alive in the Spirit, prayer groups spring up all the more. Right now in most cities, I recognize two things that are happening:

1. There are churches really ministering the healing Christ to people.
2. There are small groups meeting in different homes, who are reaching people for Christ that have not been reached before.

In addition to such prayer groups working like this together, and giving of their love to those outside, it is also good to work quietly in the church, helping permeate it with that same love and healing faith. These groups have their place but cannot take the place of the church and its worship service.

It takes some balance to do this but I see it being done.

One thing is certain, and you can depend on it, God is alive, God loves you, God is concerned about you, and God *is* going to send someone across your path with His healing power.

It's a time to be encouraged—to expect miracles, and you will get them.

Just keep Jesus in view. Focus on Him. He is your life, your abundant life.

THINGS I LEARNED ABOUT "BEING GOOD ENOUGH" TO BE HEALED

Say this:

1. I will not strike back or be bitter.

2. Jesus recognizes my humanness, and wants to heal me because I am a person.

3. I will have a positive attitude toward life and divine health—whether it comes from doctors, medication, or prayers.

4. I will keep my eyes on Jesus, my Source.

 I Know Jesus Recognizes My Humanity And Wants To Heal Me Because I Am An Important Person

Chapter 4

HOW YOU CAN FREE YOURSELF FROM THE MYTH THAT EVERY BAD THING HAPPENING TO YOU IS GOD'S PUNISHMENT

 key issue:

All Sickness Is From The Devil...All Healing Is From God—I Am Believing God For His Best

A person once wrote me and said, "Brother Roberts, I believe Jesus can heal, but I am still not well. *What is God punishing me for?*"

This kind of thinking breeds doubt, skepticism, and often bitterness toward God. It is a form of unbelief. How can we believe God to heal our sickness if we believe He sent it to us?

Some people go through life thinking that every pain, every misfortune that happens, is God punishing them. If they have an accident, God sent it. If they are sick, they are being punished. When they do not succeed, it is God's will.

I believe this is practicing negative thinking in the worst form. It is directly opposite to right believing and the proper understanding of God.

THREE MOST IMPORTANT STEPS TO YOUR BETTER HEALTH

YOUR THINKING HAS TO BE HEALED FIRST

I remember a young man we prayed for—a 28-year-old justice of the peace from Canada—afflicted with multiple sclerosis. He walked with the help of his wife and a cane. He said, "Brother Roberts, I was convinced that God was punishing me through my affliction until I heard you preach on your television program that God is a good God. I know now that He wants to heal me."

This change in his thinking was essential. For he was persuaded that God was punishing him and that he deserved it. He had to be healed in his thinking before God could heal his body. When he responded through his spirit he was able to change his thinking and start believing that God is good. The skepticism of this young man dissolved and was replaced with hope and the faith that God wanted to, and could heal him. I saw him walk without any aid whatever, and I knew the removal of the "God-is-punishing-me" myth had been important to the possibility of his full recovery.

IF GOD PUNISHED SIN WITH SICKNESS WE WOULD ALL BE SICK

If God punished sin with sickness we would all be sick. "For all (absolutely no exceptions) have sinned, and come short of the glory of God" (Romans 3:23). God does not come to put sickness on us, but He comes as the Great Physician to make us whole and well.

At the same time, we need to recognize that if we disobey God's natural laws we will suffer in our bodies.

That is, if we fail to properly care for our health, or if we indulge in anything or engage in behavior that is harmful to the body, we will suffer the negative effects of such actions. But these actions must not be blamed on God but on ourselves. We did them—God did not. God will bring only good to us if we allow Him to.

GIVE GOD'S TEMPLE—YOUR BODY—
BACK TO HIM

Singing star, Johnny Cash, who was said at one time to be taking 100 pep pills a day, says, "Every once in a while I meet someone on drugs who knows I used to be a drug addict, and he asks me what he can do to kick the habit. I tell him what I learned, 'Give God's temple back to Him!'"

The Bible says:

"What? know ye not that your body is the temple of the Holy Ghost which is in you, which ye have of God, and ye are not your own? For ye are bought with a price: therefore glorify God in your body, and in your spirit, which are God's" (1 Corinthians 6:19,20).

"The body is . . . for the Lord" (1 Corinthians 6:13).

"Present your bodies a living sacrifice, holy, acceptable unto God" (Romans 12:1).

You see, God says your body doesn't belong to you. Your body, mind, and spirit belong to God—the total you. This is why when I pray for a person I often say, "Devil, in the name of Jesus, I command you to take your hands off God's property."

God is saying your body is not made for sickness, but for health. This means that when we indulge in alcohol, cigarettes, drugs, immorality, overeating, lack of exercise, or bitterness, and other such things, we abuse and desecrate the house God lives in—our body. Again I say this is something bad we do to ourselves. We must choose, by God's help, to cease doing it and choose to replace each of these deadly negative actions by planting positive seeds of faith.

When we pay attention to our body and treat it as a sacred instrument of the Lord, it puts us in position for God to give us better health and more strength throughout our life.

GOD REMEMBERS TO FORGET

I am told of a blind man who would not ask anyone to pray for his healing because he believed God was punishing him with blindness to constantly remind him of his past sins. He believed that in some mysterious way God was getting glory out of his blindness.

This type of reasoning is contrary to God's Word. When we confess our sins and ask God's forgiveness, the Bible says He removes our sins from us as far as the east is from the west (Psalm 103:12). God does not continue to dig up our sins and try to make us "pay for them." He paid the debt for our transgressions on the cross. Now they are forgiven . . . and forgotten! The possibility of a cure for our body is in the same package with our salvation and forgiveness of sins.

A MEDICAL MIRACLE

A dear friend was slowly losing his vision. He had been a great golfer, the East Coast amateur champion. In his seventies, he still could often shoot his age.

He and his wife first came to our crusades in Phoenix in the '50s. We began to pray for his eyes. He received help that lasted another ten years. Gradually his former state of blindness returned. For reasons I don't fully understand to this day, prayer thereafter brought no further sight.

Meanwhile, his wife learned of a new technique, I think through the laser beam, where he might get his sight back. He was reluctant. Somehow he felt he had failed God in his faith. It worked once, why not again?

I faced the issue squarely. "Why," I said to him, "do you separate God's healing power? All healing power is divine."

He said, "I don't know."

I said, "But look, where do you think the doctors got their skill, where did the healing properties they use come from—is it not God who has been the Source?"

He said, "Will you pray for me again?"

I said, "Sure, and I'll pray for you if you choose to try this new laser system. To me, it's all the same, coming from the same Source—God."

A year later he came to another crusade and his wife said, "Oh, Oral and Evelyn, my husband is seeing perfectly!"

"Great!" we said, "how did it happen?"

"The operation did it. Think of it! Not only will he be able to see, but since golf has been a part of his life for 50 years he will be able to play again!"

Only a dedicated golfer knows what that means.

Every now and then when we were with them he would say, "Oral, keep my eyes in your prayers."

I believe that he reached a great understanding. He understood God had used the surgeon's skill as a part of the divine healing process for us humans. In his heart he still had his faith in God, his Source; therefore, he wanted my continuing prayers. It was evident he had come to a proper realization of how God works His healing wonders.

WHAT ABOUT PAUL'S THORN IN THE FLESH?

Occasionally someone mentions Paul's "thorn in the flesh" to me. There are numerous ways a person may suffer *in the flesh* without being sick in his body. Paul had been caught up to the third heaven where he had abundant revelations. For this reason, he was in danger of becoming puffed up. Hence, he said, "There was given to me a thorn in the flesh, *the messenger of Satan* to buffet me, lest I should be exalted above measure" (2 Corinthians 12:7).

Paul's thorn was an evil power that brought continuous physical buffetings to discourage and hinder him: weakness, persecutions, tight spots, shipwrecks, betrayals of friendship, and a long list of other opposing powers.

Paul could not understand these hindrances and he sought God three times to remove them. But God said, "No, Paul, I shall not take away this *thorn*, but I will make My strength perfect in these experiences in which you feel so weak. I will give you sufficient grace and strength to bear them victoriously" (2 Corinthians 12:9).

Through God's answer, Paul realized that in his weakness he would have to depend wholly upon God and His strength, knowledge, and power which were abundantly given to him. "Therefore," Paul said, "I take pleasure in infirmities, in reproaches, in necessities, in persecutions, in distresses for Christ's sake: for when I am weak, then am I strong" (2 Corinthians 12:10).

If this explanation of Paul's "thorn in the flesh" doesn't satisfy you, then remember this one fundamental fact: WHATEVER IT WAS, EVEN IF IT WAS SICKNESS, IT DID NOT HINDER HIM FROM BEING A FULLY ACTIVE PERSON! People I know who are ill and claim it as Paul's "thorn in the flesh" to them, are NOT fully active human beings. I know in my own personal experience with illness it hindered me every time, even to the extent of my nearly dying. *My thorn in the flesh* comes to me in forms other than sickness or disease—it comes in misunderstandings, opposition, pressures, all because of the work God has called me to do. Therefore, I must gather from God extra strength and I do this through the miracle keys of Seed-Faith, which keeps His strength flowing into me. I, too, can say with Paul, "His grace is sufficient for me" (2 Corinthians 12:9).

THE SICKNESS THAT GLORIFIES GOD

Rarely does sickness glorify God, but the Bible does record such a case. The sickness that glorifies God is the one He does not feel it is best to heal so that it may give way to a greater miracle and serve a larger purpose. This was true in the experience of Lazarus, brother of Mary and Martha.

When Lazarus fell sick his sisters sent for Jesus. The messenger said to Him, "Lord, behold, he whom thou lovest is sick." When Jesus heard that He said,

"This sickness is not unto death, but for the glory of God" (John 11:4). Jesus intended to raise Lazarus from the dead! Raising him from the dead in that special instance would glorify God more than healing him.

After Lazarus had been called forth from the grave, the Bible tells us that many of the Jews went away and believed in Jesus (John 11:45). *This is the sickness that glorifies God and it is always a special case.* I've never felt this was applicable to me or a case the Lord has had me to deal with. I leave that to Him.

GOD DOES NOT SEND SICKNESS

Do not let the devil deceive you on this point. God does not send sickness upon you. Jesus said, "The thief (devil) cometh not, but for to steal, and to kill, and to destroy: I am come that they might have life, and that they might have it more abundantly" (John 10:10). The Scriptures declare that, "For this purpose the Son of God was manifested, that he might destroy the works of the devil" (1 John 3:8).

Jesus came to bring us good, not evil. God's goodness and the works of the devil are not compatible. They are direct opposites. Sin is not righteousness; sickness is not health; poverty and affliction are not abundant life.

Jesus found among His own people those who doubted God's goodness. They questioned by whose authority He healed. In one place His critics said, "He heals by the power of Beelzebub, the chief of devils." But Jesus answered, "Every kingdom divided against itself is brought to desolation; and every city or house divided against itself shall not stand: And if Satan cast out Satan, he is divided against himself; how shall then his kingdom stand?" (Matthew 12:25,26).

Jesus was saying that if He healed sickness by the devil's power, then the devil's house was divided. In this way He showed them that His power was not from the devil but from God, who is all good. It was God's power that drove the oppression of the devil from people's bodies. "God anointed Jesus of Nazareth with the Holy Ghost and with power: who went about doing good, and *healing all that were oppressed of the devil*; for God was with him" (Acts 10:38). Healing—not sickness—glorifies God and testifies of His goodness. *Although we can glorify God while we are sick, sickness itself does not glorify God.* Whether we are sick or well, we will serve God. However, any sickness we have is no excuse to blame God.

SICKNESS IS NOT A BLESSING

It has been argued that sickness is a blessing because it draws us closer to God. If this were true, then all of us should be praying for the Lord to make us sick, because all of us want to draw closer to God. Sickness has a way of wearing you down physically, mentally, and spiritually. This is why Satan afflicts people—because he knows it is a form of oppression to their lives (Acts 10:38). It is very hard to serve God *as well* when you are sick as when you are in health. People may remain sick because they don't always know how to use their faith to get well, or because in spite of all they do the sickness seems to hold on. In many cases they don't have anyone to pray for them and help them believe for their healing. Or they don't seek the help of a competent physician or seek one who is skilled in their particular area of need. I have been with too many sick people and seen their sufferings to believe their illness was a blessing. In my own failure or futility of effort to help them, I still do not believe sickness is a way God blesses us. When I see someone suffering with no apparent hope of health again, then I must believe all the more in the RESURRECTION! For the resurrection is the greatest healing of all. (I will discuss this in detail in this same Step, Chapter 10.)

SICKNESS IS NOT A SAVING POWER

I've traveled over the world, and have found that *there is more sickness in people who are not saved than anywhere else*. If sickness is a saving power, why are not the heathen saved today? Sickness may cause a man to think upon God, but he gets saved when he knows God is good, God is available, and God is willing to give him a new life.

David, writing in Psalm 119:67, said, "Before I was afflicted I went astray; but now have I kept thy word." It is true that in a person's weakness and sickness he may realize that he needs God; and if in that sickness he comes to realize that, then he has done a good thing. This happened to me. But thousands of people realize they need God without ever getting sick. The Bible says, "THE GOODNESS OF GOD leadeth thee to repentance" (Romans 2:4). Also, "God sent not his Son into the world to *condemn* the world; but that the world through him might be saved" (John 3:17).

GOD IS NO TYRANT

A person who has grasped this great truth of the Bible wrote me:

"Brother Roberts, the wall has tumbled! Thirty-five years of fear, guilt, and mental torment which stood as insurmountable barriers between me and God have crumbled. From your teaching, I think I have—no, I KNOW I have—found the answer to my problem.

"All my life I've lived under the charge, 'You reap what you sow!' I took that the wrong way. It meant to me: 'You'd better watch out, or else!' I was afraid to approach God for forgiveness of my sins. All I could think about was how unworthy I was and how God was going to punish me.

"Through your ministry I've come to understand that a warm, joyous relationship is possible with my Savior. God is a God of love...not a tyrant. He loves me and wants me to be well and live abundantly with Him as my Source of total supply."

* * * *

Let me say this to you out of my heart. If you are struggling with the feeling that God is punishing you, tell it to the Lord. Let Him have those guilt feelings. Then accept His forgiveness and never again allow them to dominate your mind and heart. Rejoice in a GOOD God. And let the joy of knowing His goodness sweep over your spirit, and believe the power of God to make you whole.

Now, let's look at some concrete things we can do to deal with physical malfunctions and deformities.

HOW I FOUGHT AGAINST MY IMPEDIMENT AND THE CYNICISM OF PEOPLE THAT CAME WITH IT

The terrible impediment of speech with which I was born was bad enough for me to bear. In some ways it was worse to face the cynical attitude of people who took delight (fiendish delight, it seemed to me) in teasing me.

Not only did they enjoy hearing me stutter and laughing at me, but never once did they indicate by any action that I could overcome my stuttering.

My mother and father were the only ones who gave me evidence on which to build hope. Mamma said, "Oral, some day you *will* talk. God will loose your tongue and you'll preach the gospel."

Papa told an uncle who had thought I never would amount to anything, "Oh, yes, he will. He's going to preach the gospel."

My uncle said, "Oral, preach? Why, he can't even talk." And he burst out laughing.

Both Mamma and Papa tied my cure from stuttering, to God AND to a purpose for my life which, for *me,* happened to be God's call on my life to preach the gospel.

Whatever your impediment is—stuttering, or something else—the best way I know for you to come into faith for overcoming it is to put God squarely in your thoughts as the Source of your new freedom, AND to tie *your* inner self to a positive goal, something you feel deeply inside and then work toward it with all your might.

This seems to release the adrenalin in your system, also it makes God more real to you, who in turn *releases* direct healing power toward your problem.

THE HEALING TOUCH OF GOD IS POWERFUL

I was born a stutterer. I stuttered when I first learned to talk. The more I fought it, the more I stuttered and the more frightened I became that I would stutter. In looking back at it I would estimate that 20 percent of it was a physical impediment and 80 percent was rooted in fear.

When I was with my parents or my brother Vaden, with whom I grew up in a very close relationship, I stuttered very little. When I grew tense or was afraid, I couldn't say the words. When I was caught off guard and asked a question which required me to reply, I stuttered. The more I was removed from familiar things, the more I was unable to talk—the words freezing in my throat.

When Elmer carried me for prayer for my healing of tuberculosis, the presence of God filled my being. It touched both my physical being and my inner self. I could breathe all the way down, *and* I could talk!

The strongest, the most exhilarating, the most positive force I have ever felt is the presence of God. You feel so strong, so capable, you feel you can do anything (and you just about can). Through the healing presence of Christ I see people walk that couldn't walk. I see them coming out of wheelchairs, their bones creaking, their bodies trembling, but when their feet touch the floor they start walking, getting stronger every step. I see people who can't hear well, or breathe well, gathering a new power to be free from those impediments.

It's the healing presence of God!

Not enough people understand that they can experience God's healing presence. Many who believe in it do not expect to feel it often and powerful enough. Others are cynical, critical, opposed, not realizing they are hurting themselves *and other dear people*.

MORE ON IMPEDIMENTS

Medical research and developments are doing God's wonders with many impediments today such as hairlip, facial and body disfigurements, tooth and gum problems, hip displacements, etc. I couldn't begin to name them all since new breakthroughs are appearing every year.

In addition, we who pray for the sick sometimes see short legs lengthened. I recently witnessed a cancerous growth literally fall off a person's ear.

It's an exciting time to be a believer. To begin to know in your spirit that God is concerned about you as a person, and as an individual, is exhilarating. To know you can do something toward getting healed through prayer AND have hope of so much being done medically for you, is a cause for rejoicing.

Just don't get mixed up on who your Source is. If you keep God as the Source of your better health, you can accept prayer or medicine or both with equal humility, and appreciation. You can be grateful for those instruments but know in your heart that God is the Source of your healing, and your continuing better health.

Now say to yourself:

"I HAVE FREED MYSELF FROM THE MYTH—'GOD IS PUNISHING ME' "

1. If God punished sin with sickness we would all be sick.

2. My body is the temple of God; therefore, I will take care of it through right believing, right food, and proper exercise —I will give it back to Him.

3. Jesus paid the debt for my salvation AND my healing.

4. There is only one sickness that glorifies God—the one that gives way to a greater miracle (John 11:4).

5. God does not send sickness to me— He sent Jesus to destroy it (1 John 3:8) and that includes sickness in any form it takes.

6. Sickness is not a saving power (Romans 2:4).

7. God is not a tyrant, He is a God of love. He loves me and wants me to live abundantly.

HOW I FOUGHT MY IMPEDIMENT AND THE CYNICISM OF PEOPLE THAT CAME WITH IT

1. I will put God squarely in my thoughts.

2. I will visualize the healing presence of God.

3. I will take advantage of what medical science can do for me.

 key issue: *All Sickness Is From The Devil...All Healing Is From God—I Am Believing God For His Best*

Chapter 5

HOW YOU CAN KNOW GOD LOVES YOU SO MUCH THAT HE WILL HEAL YOU EVEN THOUGH YOU HAVEN'T BELIEVED HE WOULD

 key issue: **I Will Not "Fake It" About Any Illness — I Will "Faith It" Through To Healing**

(This is an exciting testimony of Dr. James Buskirk, a very dear friend and the Dean of the Oral Roberts University Graduate School of Theology.)

As I drove the 85 miles back from the specialist, his words burned in my mind, "I'm sorry, but in six months you will be blind..."

And I remember thinking, that means my ministry is over...

I was so threatened by the doctor's diagnosis, I was afraid to tell the people in my church that I was losing my eyesight. I was afraid they wouldn't want me anymore.

I loved the ministry and I loved my people so I decided to fake it as long as possible.

When I could no longer see to read the Scriptures I'd memorize them by listening to tapes. And then when I'd get up to preach I'd hold up my Bible and pretend that I was reading, when really I had memorized it.

I spent many tedious hours in the church sanctuary memorizing the steps from the back of the church to the pulpit. In time, I could move from the lectern into the pulpit and take the offering and put it on the high altar—all with my eyes closed. I moved with studied ease. I didn't want to stumble for fear that someone would suspect that something was wrong. But the Lord doesn't always let us get by with our ways—He usually has a better way.

He used a lady in the church whose spiritual maturity threatened me at the time. She had a prayer group that really bugged me. They invited me one time to come and give the devotion for their group. And in the course of my talk I said in real nice pastoral language, "If you ladies would put some legs on your prayers, I'd believe in your praying more. . ."

To which this lady answered, "Brother Jimmy, if you'd learn how to pray, you'd stop running your legs off. . ."

One day she came into my office and said, "Brother Jimmy, what's the matter with you?"

She really took me off guard, but I knew how to dodge so I said, "Why do you ask?"

And she said, "Well, you keep me awake at night. Sometimes I wake up and I pray for you for a whole hour before I can go back to sleep."

I really didn't understand this. Then she said, "If you're going to keep me awake, I've got a right to know what's the matter with you."

Well, I was just floored and I said, "Well, I've got a cold. . ."

To which she replied, "Oh, *hell*! Jimmy, I want to know what is *really* the matter with you." She obviously was a person who couldn't tolerate sham and could spot a phony a mile away.

And I thought, O, Lord, if she's really such a saint, it looks like You'd clean up her language. But, really, I was kind of glad that she had a problem. You see, I didn't use that kind of language and I wanted to be *ahead* of her somewhere. My mother taught me as a very small child never to use rough language or to take the name of the Lord in vain, "Because," she said, "if you take His name in vain now, He may not hear you when you call on Him in earnest." So it was deep in my consciousness never to use rough language.

I knew this woman had never had a day of counseling and I knew she wouldn't be able to handle my problem. So I decided to just drop the whole thing on her and watch her reaction. And so I said, "I AM GOING BLIND."

Well, it didn't upset her a bit. It kind of made me mad. It was *my eyes* that I was talking about and I wanted her to get upset at least a little. But, instead, she just said in a very matter-of-fact way, "I'm not sure that's going to happen. We're going to pray . . ."

And she wasn't asking—she just started praying. I don't think I'll ever forget her prayer. She said:

"Lord, we know You always heal Your own, sometimes here and sometimes in the resurrection . . ."

I thought, I don't believe that. I've known good people who died. But that "sometimes in the resurrection" really hit me. "Sometimes here and sometimes in the resurrection . . ."

And again, I thought, that's not fair.

But she went on, "Lord, we're not telling You what to do or when to do it. That's Your program and Your calendar. But I just pray that You will help Brother Jimmy to trust Your fantastic love so much that he can accept the healing already in process. Lord, we just praise You."

And just as abruptly as she walked in, she walked out, closed the door, and shut me up in there with God. And I began to pray—I mean I really prayed. I said, "God, I thought I'd given You all of me. Maybe I've never given my eyes to You, so it has occurred to me, Lord, that maybe I've never given You my ministry either. I've been terribly concerned about the fact that I was going to lose it, and I've begged You to give it back to me. But, Lord, I *really* GIVE You my ministry, and whatever I have from this point on I claim as a bonus—as a gift from You."

But even then, I didn't really surrender. I wanted to—but somehow I didn't have the strength, the surrender power. It was at this point that God used my dad.

My father was a United Methodist minister. I grew up in Methodist parsonages and Dad and I were close. But I could communicate better with my mother. She and I can sometimes communicate even without talking. The problem was, Dad wanted me to preach but I was determined not to preach unless my *Heavenly* Father called me to preach—not my earthly father. So there was a time when Dad and I grew a little bit apart. And I suppose I stayed closer to Mother longer because of this.

But Dad came to my office one day alone, which was a little unusual. He came in and said:

"Mother's down at the house."

I said, "Great, let's go."

He said, "No. I carried her down there for a reason. I wanted to come here alone. I want to talk to you and I don't want any response except 'yes.'"

He sounded serious. Then he started, "I've got only one year left in this ministry before I retire, and you've got your whole lifetime in front of you. I want you to call Doctor McKinney in Memphis and tell him we will come anytime he says. Tell him I want him to take my eyes and put them in your head. And I want him to give me your eyes. You've got peripheral vision and that's enough for me to see to get around. With my eyes you can continue your ministry . . ."

Here I am the professional minister who knows how to deal with all kinds of things suddenly coming apart as I hear my father's words. Stalling, I turned around to get a book out of the bookcase behind me. Then I said, "Dad, I'm faking it. I don't need this book . . . but I think I'm about to come apart . . . would you let me be alone for just a little while."

He left and I put my head down on my desk and I didn't just *pray*, "Lord, I give You my ministry," that time. I *really did give it to Him*. I realized that all my begging God to give me back my sight was not really faith. It was lack of faith. I was trying to *convince* God. And suddenly I realized if my earthly father wanted me to have my vision so much he'd give me his eyes, that I could afford to trust whatever God would do for me, because my dad's love is just a reflection of my Heavenly Father's love. And my vision started returning from that point. It returned gradually within about a year.

I went back to my specialist and after examining me he said, "You know, we've been concerned about your other eye going fast, but the eye that we'd given up on is being restored."

Then he said, "I know you've memorized the chart, so read it backwards . . ."

I read it backwards and then I said, "Do you want me to read the chart or those little numbers by the side?"

He said, "Can you see those? That takes better than 20-20 vision!"

And I said, "How do you explain this?"

And he said, "You're a minister and you're asking me? Why, son, God and I have been in business together for years. I treat and He heals. The medicine I gave you may have arrested the infection. But whatever sight you have, the Great Physician gave you *that* and you ought to thank Him every morning . . ."

And I do.

What a theology that doctor taught me! All healing is from God—He just uses different instruments. Sometimes it's through medicine, sometimes it's through surgery, sometimes through love and prayer. In my case it was my own father and the lady in my church who reflected God's healing love to me through prayer, and of course my doctor.

HOW YOU CAN REFLECT ON DR. BUSKIRK'S HEALING

1. I will no longer fake it about any illness I have.

2. I will make myself open to any instrument God sends to me.

3. Any part of me I have not given to God, I humbly do it now.

4. If a loved one, like Dr. Buskirk's father, would offer his own eyes to his son, how much more does God offer me His own life and health.

5. For every gift of God's healing power coming to me through prayer or medical help, I will give God thanks—daily.

 key issue:

I Will Not "Fake It" About Any Illness—I Will "Faith It" Through To Healing

Chapter 6

WHILE YOU ARE IN YOUR HUMAN SKIN YOU CAN STILL BREAK THROUGH TO GOD'S DIVINE HEALING POWER

 key issue: **I Have A "Faith Miracle" In Me Every Second And I Will Accept It**

Jesus Christ wore a human skin exactly like yours. His body had the same organic structure. He wore clothes. He lived in houses. He ate at the tables of friends and family. He worked, bathed, slept. At times He lived outdoors. He walked the dusty roads of the Holy Land, climbed its mountains, worked at physical fitness. He read the Scriptures, attended God's house, and learned from God the ideas to apply to His humanness. He laughed, cried, sighed, angered, whispered, shouted, tensed, strained, rested, relaxed. He was admired, adored, worshiped, loved. He was opposed, ridiculed, criticized, brutalized, discriminated against, on occasion denied a place to sleep or rest. He slipped away to relax, to pray, to meditate, to replenish himself inwardly and outwardly. In all these things He got in tune with life, with people, with God and himself. He had a goal and He stuck with it.

When I was studying the Four Gospels and The Acts back there in 1947, I saw Him just as I have described Him. That fresh new look that I took of Him caused me to see Him:

(1) as a man just as I am a man,
(2) as the Savior and Source who helps me
to become the man God wants me to be
while I am in the same kind of skin He was in.
I got excited about this
and still am. I glimpsed the
possibility of total health.

YOU HAVE A FAITH MIRACLE IN YOU EVERY SECOND

You have this possibility. What you must do about it is another thing. That means you must get an attitude for this faith miracle.

How do you do this?

Do it like Jesus did it while He wore a human skin. He was always fighting against fear. He said, "Fear not" and, "Don't be afraid." He said this to help others, but it was also a seed He planted to help himself *not* to be fearful or afraid.

Jesus had a lot of things to be afraid of, and had He allowed himself to become terrified by any of them, then fear would have destroyed Him as it would destroy any of us. By resisting fear He was able to move right into faith, and when He got into faith there was the instant possibility of a faith miracle happening to Him or through Him. I personally try to live in an attitude that this same possibility *of a faith miracle* can happen in me, and through me, as it did Jesus. I've taught it to many others. I'm teaching it to you now.

In my human skin, in which I live 24 hours a day, I fight against fear. It attacks me on every side. Sometimes it keeps me awake. Sometimes I wake up in a cold sweat.

Sometimes it gnaws at my stomach and makes me ill. But through Christ, who I know experienced it before me, I will not have it. I will not be afraid. I will have faith in God. God made me able to believe and have faith, the same as He has you. He has given each of us a full measure of faith (Romans 12:3). It is not something we have to get, we already have it.

If you think you don't have any faith, I'm going to show you that you do. Every time you step into a car to go somewhere, that is faith. You can transfer that same kind of faith into your inner self and respond to life with your spirit—which is the way God made you and intended for you to respond. It's in this way that you can understand that faith is something *you do*.

HAVE YOU PRESSED THE BUTTON?

I heard about a group of people standing before a public elevator. When the door didn't open, they began to say, "Why doesn't somebody do something? Isn't it terrible the way things are?"

Then a voice from the edge of the crowd asked, "Has anybody pushed the button?"

No. They had not.

What I am trying to say is that simple faith is a necessary thing, something you *do* every day of your life.

But it is the same in using your faith to believe in God, to believe against sin, disease, demons, fear, and ALL self-defeating, self-limiting forces coming against you.

It is really faith that causes you to push an elevator button to cause the door to open, to close, and for the elevator to rise. The kind of faith you use to get in cars and elevators and other things is the same as spiritual faith. There really is no difference in simple faith and spiritual faith, they *both* happen when you do something that must be done.

The elevator button to be pushed is the *Point of Contact* which sets off the electronic circuit to make your elevator go into action. These spiritual "buttons" are to be pushed, as points of contact for the release of your faith which, in turn, sets in motion toward you all God's healing good!

But don't expect something for nothing. Don't expect God to overwhelm your power of choice and force His miracles on you. The elevator doesn't do that, does it? *You* push the button.

There are specific ways God wants you to live and specific things He wants you to do which will cause His abundant life to flow toward you.

I believe the miracles of Jesus are coming TOWARD YOU, OR PAST YOU every day! You must use your faith to believe God is sending these miracles toward you and not past you. You must believe God wants you to have miracles, and reach out and take them.

WHAT I HAVE LEARNED ABOUT HAVING TOTAL HEALTH WHILE I AM IN MY HUMAN SKIN

Now say these things to yourself:

1. **I can learn to be more like Jesus was while He was on earth in human skin— I can have health too.**

2. **The Key Issue is: *"I have a 'faith miracle' in me every second and I will accept it."***

3. I will not fear, but work on moving into a faith attitude.

4. In my human skin I will fight against all negative forces coming aginst me, because God has given me a full measure of faith to fight with.

5. I will press the faith button on my spiritual elevator to make it rise to my highest expectation for miracle-living.

6. Miracles are coming toward me, or past me, every day! I will reach out and take mine.

7. Jesus lived in His human skin successfully and I am determined to do the same.

 key issue:

I Have A "Faith Miracle" In Me Every Second And I Will Accept It

Chapter 7

NOW TO SUCCESSFULLY DEAL WITH YOUR DEADLY NEGATIVE EMOTIONS

 key issue:

I Am Looking For New Dimensions For My Faith And Love To Shine Through To Others

One thing I am sure of about myself is that I am an emotional *being*. Not necessarily an emotional *person* since I manage to keep myself pretty well under control, but an emotional *being*. There is a difference.

Built into our very nature are our emotions, our ability to feel, to respond, or react. When you respond you are usually positive and in control of what you wish to do—or be. When you react you are permitting the other person—or whatever it is bugging you—to determine your actions. Now I don't like to do that. No person or thing should be allowed to have so much control over us as to force us to react in a negative way. We really hurt ourselves when we do that.

I'll never forget staying with a family whose little 4-year-old son who when he was reprimanded, or he hurt himself, or if anything happened he didn't like, would rush to the brick fireplace and butt his head against the wall. His little head was battered and blue.

I've done that, only in a different way. Presumably you have too.

Isn't there a better way to deal with our negative emotions?

BLESS OR CURSE

I remember one day that one of our attorneys told me about a pretty bad experience he'd had with a fellow lawyer. And he said, "Oral, you know what I said to him?"

I said, "No."

He said, "I told him to go to hell."

"Did you mean it?"

"Sure, I meant it."

"Do you know what hell is?" I asked . . . "Hell is a separation from God. Hell is a place of torment. You didn't really want him to go to hell, did you?"

"Well, since you put it that way—no; I really didn't want that. I just wanted him to get out of my sight."

And I said, "Well, then why didn't you tell him to go to heaven?"

"Go to heaven? I didn't want him to go to heaven."

"Well, heaven is a good place. It's where everything is right in a man's life. Wouldn't you like for things to be right with him?"

He said, "Well, I sure wish he would get right some way or other."

I didn't hear anything more from him and a few weeks later I saw him again and he said, "Oral, you know, I have been thinking a lot about what you said to me about telling that guy to go to heaven. And every time I've started to tell someone to go to hell, I've caught myself. Once I even told a guy to go to heaven and, you know, he really didn't know how to take it."

Later he saw me, came over, and said with a smile, "Tell him to go to heaven! You know you really cleaned up my language and something deeper than that."

I've used this approach with many people whose emotions play fast and loose with bad language and bad thoughts. Almost all turn out to be grateful.

SAY, "GOD BLESS YOU"

The late Thelma Shaw, beloved wife of Judge Oras Shaw, dear friends to Evelyn and me, once told us she used the "God-bless-you" approach when her emotions began getting her into *reaction*. She said, "I would breathe a little prayer, sort of take a breath and say *of them* to myself, "God bless you." Over the years she developed this as a *response* and at her death when the Judge invited me to say a few words, I shared this with the audience. To my surprise, people all over the church were nodding their heads, remembering this about her. Obviously, many there had been helped by this terrific Christian woman.

We had the honor of printing her story, "God bless you," in our quarterly publication, DAILY BLESSING, in the April-May-June 1971 issue. Hundreds wrote of the good impact it had made on them.

Let me tell you that a naked, raw, uncontrolled or misdirected emotion can hurt people, and certainly yourself most of all. To deal with it you can replace it with something better. You can and you must.

IN BEING PRAYED FOR OR TREATED, WATCH YOUR NEGATIVE EMOTIONS

Richard, my son, and I played a game of golf one day with a Tulsa surgeon who had as his guest a surgeon friend who had expressed a desire to play a round with us. We played a few holes before we got to talking about the kind of people who respond or react to recovering from some illness or bad situation. He had heard me on television and knew quite well what I thought about this kind of thing.

He said, "Dr. Roberts, let me bring something very important to your attention. The worst kind of case to get in surgery is the fellow who's been in an accident and you are called to rush over to the emergency room and if necessary do quick surgery on him. First, he doesn't want to be there. Next, he's upset that he's injured. Then he doesn't know me, I'm a stranger to him. Also, he's afraid something is hurt real bad or he's going to die."

I asked, "What does he usually do?"

"Well," he replied, "he looks at me with a look that says, 'What am I doing here? Why did this happen to me? What's this doctor up to? I wish I were a million miles from here'."

"What do you do?"

"What do I do? Brother, the best I can. If I can calm him down, help get his emotions under control, and if I can give him my very best, often he comes out of it as good as ever."

"And if you can't get his emotions down?"

"Well, I try first of all to have mine under control because I am in a hot spot myself. I don't know him, I may have an impossible case on my hands, I may even get sued. Then as best I can I seek to show him how to help me help him."

A WILD MAN ACCOSTS US

I told this surgeon about a service in which I was ministering to the sick when a man leaped up and came through the audience jumping over people until he reached the stage. Four men grabbed him but couldn't control him. He got close enough to me until I saw his eyes seemed glazed. He was actually a man, berserk, and his strength was unnaturally great. I said to the ORU chaplain, Bob Stamps, who was also seeking to restrain the man, to turn him loose.

I said, "Come over here to me."

He did, and I said, "Put your arms around my neck and tell me you love me."

A hush had fallen over the place. The young man put his arms around me, laid his cheek to mine, and whispered, "Brother Roberts, I love you."

I said, "Are you ready to go back to your seat and wait your turn to come with the others for prayer?"

He said, "Yes."

"Go then," I said, and he did.

Bob said, "President Roberts, I'm glad that was you instead of me."

I smiled, "Bob, I've been down the path for nearly 30 years. It makes a difference. However, anyone can do this WHEN his own emotions are under the control of the Holy Spirit."

I told the doctor that story. He said, "Well, you put it in terms that *you* understand, and I in mine, but hopefully it works out the same way."

I said, "Yes, I believe it is very important to you, to me, to everyone, to let the *inner calm* take over — and I believe those we seek to help have to come under the same emotional control, however hard it is."

One dear woman I prayed for was accompanied by her husband. She talked incessantly. Each time I attempted to guide her into prayer, off she would go again. I nor her husband could do anything.

I felt the Holy Spirit flow up in me and I said forceably, "Stop."

She flinched like she had been struck. "Just stop," I repeated quietly, "and let God have a chance to say something to your spirit."

She hushed. We prayed. In moments she was so helped that her husband said, "God has given me a new wife."

If you want help from a minister, a doctor, or someone able to help you, try to cooperate in a positive manner. If you didn't need help, you wouldn't be there. You may be pleasantly surprised at the wonders of your recovery.

HOW ABOUT YOUR BITTERNESS?

"Lest any root of bitterness springing up trouble you, and thereby . . . be defiled . . ." (Hebrews 12:15).

Bitterness springs from a root. *A root is from something planted.*

I used to say, "Oh, he made me so bitter." God revealed to me in this Scripture and others in the Bible that my bitterness was not forced on me by someone else. I did it. I let it happen. I had planted a bad seed by permitting myself to become bitter.

One man had especially been awful to me. I fought and fought with myself, calling on God to H-E-L-P him and to H-E-L-P me. Finally, I fell upon a wonderful plan. It was to think not of the wrongs I felt he was doing to me. Instead, I tried to think of Christ in Him, and I prayed to the Christ in him who was also in me. I actually did this several times. *"O Lord, You are in this man and You are in me. I call upon You; help him; help me."* In one of these prayers I felt a release in my spirit. The wrongs were still there but they didn't hurt me anymore. I felt better and BETTER until I felt God whisper in my heart, "If you trust Me, no one can ever hurt you. You can only hurt yourself by planting the seed of a bad reaction."

I use this plan often and it works. It works because all of God's children are part of Christ, and part of one another. You and I are sowing our seed and reaping it back when we pray to Christ who is in us. The help we ask for the other person is a seed that comes back MULTIPLIED like any other Seed-Faith we plant. This has an amazing health effect upon our entire being. Frankly, I think it's part of better health and it certainly leads to miracle-living. Will you try it?

RESENTMENTS . . .

When you are in the public, as I am, they can write good stories about you—also unflattering ones. Of course you eat up the good ones and hope your emotions will not get you down over the bad ones. The fact is the bad ones are as good as the good ones because in the long run you need *balance*. As St. Paul said, not to think more highly of ourselves than we ought (Romans 12:3).

But in the short run—it's tough to keep our emotions under control.

Several years ago an unflattering article was written about my ministry, and the man responsible was a friend of mine. It really hurt me and I was angry. Very angry.

I honestly tried to overcome the resentment. The resentment I had in my heart was worse than what this man had done to me. And every time I thought about that man I got a sick feeling in the pit of my stomach. And my *attitude* was hindering me in dealing with other people.

Finally, I realized it wasn't that I had the anger—the anger had me! I began praying about it and one day I felt God speaking deep inside me, "Oral, write this man a letter and apologize for your feelings." What! I thought. He should apologize to me! But God kept telling me I had to love the man as if he'd never wronged me.

So I sat down to write the letter. And it was hard. I told him I'd felt bad toward him and I asked him to forgive me for it. When I mailed the letter I was released from the anger. *I considered this act a seed of faith I was planting for my feelings to change.* This was the desired result for which I planted my seed. And it happened. I felt great and was able to dismiss the whole thing from my mind.

Then lo and behold! A few days later here came a reply from the man, saying, "I am the one who needs to apologize . . ." We were reconciled and today he and I are good friends. But even if he had not replied, the RESENTMENT was released in my inner man and I received a healing in my spirit. Again, the Seed-Faith prayer and the Seed-Faith letter I wrote had paid off for me—and him.

WHEN PEOPLE WON'T PAY WHAT THEY OWE YOU . . .

Suppose that you have done everything legal and proper to collect—and fail. Talk about emotions running wild. Some people have fist fights, or knife someone, or even kill. Others burn and seethe inside.

It helps me to feel better in situations like these when I can get quiet enough to remember a debt I owe

AND CAN NEVER PAY. I owe Christ everything for dying on the cross for me.

Bringing that down to wages, or money loaned, or other favors rendered, it's important to remember WHO YOUR SOURCE IS.

An associate of mine who believes in Seed-Faith living as I do, told me of an amount of money he had foolishly lost. He had signed a note for a friend when he knew the friend might not seriously try to pay him back. "I knew better," he said, "but the fellow got on my sympathy."

He said, "Oral, he just wouldn't pay and I had to go pay it myself by going to the bank and borrowing it! Every time I'd make a payment to the bank, I'd be taking something from my family, and the thoughts I had toward this man were more bitter than gall. It made me sick to my stomach."

I said, "You actually felt it physically?"

He said, "Yes."

"Well, you look OK now."

"I am. I am fine. In your book, MIRACLE OF SEED-FAITH, you said something about giving a loss to Christ as seed you plant, and in that way God would multiply the seed back and it would wipe out the loss."

I replied, "Yes, I said that and I try to practice it."

He said, "I was desperate to keep my emotions from eating me up, from harming myself with all those bad feelings I was harboring. I prayed for this man, I prayed for myself, then I mentally took that loss, all of it, and gave it to God. As I paid the rest of the bank payments I thought only of giving it to God and God has multiplied it back 100 percent and more."

"You won then?"

"Yes, I won by getting myself released so I could apply myself to more worthwhile things. It's been multiplied in money and peace of mind."

Wonderful things happen to people who can finally get themselves opened up from resentment by getting into Seed-Faith, which can wipe out the loss.

THE EMOTION OFTEN MOST NEGATIVE IS SELF-PITY...

We are all afflicted at times with this one. Even the stoical often seethe within because they feel they are not getting treated fairly. We have every right to feel appreciated, wanted, loved. But it appears impossible for other people to see us as we feel they should.

Self-pity hits me worse when I have worked hard and given of myself until I am worn out in my body and maybe can't sleep well for a few nights. Or I pick up what somebody I admire has said, which is negative toward me. Or I take a cold that gets worse and goes into something else like a sore throat or a hurting chest. The throat and chest are vital to a speaker—one who has to talk and share vocally with people, both publicly and privately. Some people can go home and rest until it's all over; we can't. The work of television, prayers for people, ministering to individuals and large groups keeps us from stopping. So I have to constantly fight feelings of self-pity.

Of course my darling wife Evelyn helps me. "Now, Oral," she will say, "you're just feeling sorry for yourself. You tell others wonderful things to help them, try them on yourself." She is right and this really snaps me to attention, because self-pity can destroy all God wants us to be.

HATE . . . HOW JESUS KEPT HIS EMOTIONS UNDER CONTROL

Many a person is behind prison bars because of permitting his emotions to go into hate until he did something violent. Every prison I have visited struck me as being filled with a hate you could feel.

I recall speaking in a large church once and I felt like a lot of hate was there also. How could hate be in a church? People. People who planted bad seed by misdirecting their emotions and becoming deadly negative toward each other. In that situation I prayed while I preached that the Living Christ would speak through me and that the people would *feel* His love in me. Later the pastor of that church told me that something happened to his people through that sermon, and especially through what they felt coming out of me toward them. I realized that the good seed I had planted in my sermon had been multiplied in blessings to the people, and back to me also.

You know, it's so true that what people feel coming out of you is as important as what they hear you say. This is true in sermons, I know, as was proved in this case.

If any human being ever had a reason to feel hate, it was Jesus. The very ones He sought to help, rejected Him. Ultimately they wanted to take His life.

Being rejected and hated was no picnic even to Jesus because He was fully human. I hope you remember He was *man*, an emotional being like yourself.

The thing that helps me most is that in the midst of their hate, Jesus could call upon His inner man and respond from His spirit, rather than from the cold calculating logic of His mind, which would have caused Him to hate them back.

243

Jesus resisted hate. He determined not to hate. It was a battle for Him to win over himself just as it is for us. He won by planting seeds of His love for them.

I believe Jesus loved all people but He loved himself too. He knew that hate, like acid, can do damage to the vessel in which it is stored just as it does to the object on which it is poured. Hatred, He knew, can blind your reason, send poison into your bloodstream, upset your digestive system, make your head hurt, cause you to be irritable—it can punish you until all you think of is punishing someone else. It is a bad, bad seed and the hater gets his seed multiplied back in hate for himself.

How did you do it, Jesus? I often ask. In studying His life, and in observing Him working in my life, I have concluded that *love* sown as a seed of faith *is* the answer.

A love that is toward God. A love that is toward the person. A love that is toward yourself. "Love your neighbor as you love yourself," Jesus said. He is saying, "Plant the *good* seed, not the bad."

"AS YOU LOVE YOURSELF." Loving others also means *not* hating yourself. You are on the same plane as other people are. You have self-worth, you *are* somebody. God is very aware of you and values you as highly as He does anyone! After all, He died for you! So plant a good seed in behalf of yourself. God wants you to do it.

MY MOTHER HELPED ME

Once I came home from another country where we came close to death for preaching the gospel and praying for the sick. I sat down with my dear mother and told her all about it. The news had preceded me. as newspaper reporters had phoned to get her comments. She had proudly said to them, "I am proud of my son, proud he is a preacher, an evangelist, and is doing what God called him to do. I raised him to obey God." Then she added, "There's only one like him in the world and I gave him birth."

One reporter later told me that after talking with my mother he was going to give me objective reporting thereafter. "Why?" I asked. "Well," he replied, "anybody with a mother like her has got to be all right."

I recounted to my mother that experience overseas, how the great crowds came, and of the tremendous results in conversions and healings. Then of the final overwhelming of the services by hoodlums, with no protection for us by the officers of the law who were standing by with their arms folded. And I noticed a softness came into her eyes. She said, "Oral, your daddy and I have carried the gospel since before you were born. We went through heat and cold, plenty and starvation, praise and hatred—but we carried on. We've taught you about Jesus and how He never struck back with bitterness or hate or revenge. Just remember this about those who tried to harm you; God knows all about it. Also consider the source of their opposition, the devil. Keep your trust in God and He will bring you through. Some day you will come through it all shining like the stars, and you'll be glad, oh, so glad that you never struck back . . ."

As I reflect today I know Mamma is right. I can see the stars shining and I feel gladness in my heart. Not once in all the years of this ministry have I struck back at anyone. There were inner thoughts and emotions I wrestled with. Privately I was terribly upset, again and again. But I could feel Jesus in my soul, the same Jesus who suffered ten thousand times more than I have. I can see Him and hear Him on the cross, "Father, forgive . . ."

Loving forgiveness is the seed to plant to wipe hatred from your heart. One thing about a farmer planting a seed, he's doing something constructive, not something destructive. He's planting his seed for a desired result. When you see Jesus' own way of forgiving, you see He is doing something constructive. He is seeing to it that the seed He is planting is the seed of forgiveness, not the seed of destruction of those who are against Him. When you see this then you know the only seed you will plant are seeds of love and goodness. In this way, you never harm anyone and it comes back to you multiplied again and again.

Oh, that we might study our Savior's actions more, and better learn how to love, how to forgive, and how to have the superior health He had in spirit, mind, and body, and in all His relationships with people.

SOMETHING GOOD IS GOING TO HAPPEN TO YOU

Those words with which I open all our television programs and which I use with people wherever I go, were born in my heart when bad things were happening to me. Back in 1968 through a misunderstanding by some of my friends and partners over my change in church denominations (which God guided me to make), my ministry began to suffer quick and severe losses. I had to borrow money to make our payroll and it appeared even ORU would go under.

I had served people, thousands of them. I had given of myself, I knew that beyond any doubt. Many good and powerful things had happened through me and through this ministry. Now what I considered an obedience to God became a rallying point to those who put denomination above obeying God.

After much suffering and loss, I came to a decision. I would continue obeying God as He gave me the light. I would not strike back. I would not reply in kind to the large number of negative letters I received from former close friends in high and low places. Rather, I would answer each letter as a seed of my faith and love — and I would trust God as my SOURCE.

Looking back and seeing the great things God has done through this ministry since then, more than quadrupling our work with people who have needs it seems such a light thing I was experiencing. It was not light then, however. It was a rough and a potentially destructive period in my life.

What finally happened was that I was able to plant a seed for an equal benefit. It began with my examining my beliefs about Seed-Faith giving, and I found them fully scriptural and 100 percent workable. I made up my mind I would go to the Prayer Tower here on the ORU campus, close myself in with God, and work my way so deeply into Seed-Faith that I would come out of this with my faith intact, and leave the results with God. If I won, I won; if I failed, I failed. It would be in God's hands.

A short time later we had an offer to sell a large piece of equipment no longer needed, and we desperately needed the money to tide us over a few more days. While praying I felt a deep urge to give it rather than sell it. I felt like planting a seed. I tested that urge by seeing if it was a mere whim soon to pass or a true move of the Spirit within that wouldn't leave me.

The urge stayed with me until it was like an old friend. A knowing filled my heart and I knew that I knew that I knew. This is the way I always know it is God telling me to plant my seeds of faith. It has never failed me.

To give that piece of valuable equipment was giving OUT OF OUR NEED. It was also giving for a desired result from God, our Source. Yes, we did give it and it opened me up in my spirit, getting me beyond my intellect and my physical senses. After we had planted our seed of faith, I felt these words coming out of my innermost being . . .

Something

      good

         is

           going

              to

                 happen

                    to

                       you!

"Something good is going to happen to me, Lord?" I asked. "Yes, to you," swelled up in my heart.

The good that happened was that all I had known about planting a seed of faith and expecting God to multiply it back by a miracle, came to a climax in my thinking and believing. It gave me the push I needed to launch completely into Seed-Faith with my whole being: *To give God my best, then ask Him for His best.* I had been doing that all the years of my ministry; however, now I saw I could do it better, more consistently, more joyously, and with a greater expectation for miracles. It was another turning point in myself as a person and as a spiritual leader.

Almost overnight we developed the new television format we have continually refined until today millions say it with me, "Something good is going to happen to you . . . to me!"

People write and tell me, "Brother Roberts, you will never know what it means to me to hear you say, 'Something good is going to happen to you.' It lifts me up, it cheers me on, it gives me reason for living, it brings me closer to God . . ."

It does the same for me.

A friend wrote that his 90-year-old mother had gotten up one Sunday morning and came into the living room where on their TV set I was saying, "Something good is going to happen to you."

He said his mother wiped the sleep out of her eyes, gave a little lift to her head, and said, "Let 'er happen, sonny."

I tell you, that kind of up-attitude certainly is a boon to your emotional being.

THINGS I HAVE LEARNED TO DO ABOUT DEADLY NEGATIVE EMOTIONS

Say them with me:

1. I know that I am an emotional being— how I act or react is important to me, and to others. It is a good seed planted or a bad seed planted.

2. Bitterness and resentments within come from a bad seed planted—therefore, I will not let any root of bitterness spring up (Hebrews 12:15). I will plant good seed.

3. I will give my losses to God as a seed of faith I plant and let God multiply the seed back, wiping out the loss.

4. I will not indulge in self-pity...it can destroy all God wants me to be.

5. I will plant seeds of love toward people instead of hate.

 key issue:

I Am Looking For New Dimensions For My Faith And Love To Shine Through To Others

Chapter 8

HOW TO UNDERSTAND WHEN YOU NEED A PHYSICIAN AND SUGGESTIONS ON HOW AND WHEN TO GO TO A DOCTOR

 key issue: **God Uses Prayer And Physicians To Complete His Healing Love In Me**

Jesus said, "They that are sick . . . need a physician."

First, in understanding that you need a physician, learn to appreciate a man or woman who has spent hard years in preparation to be a physician or dentist. What a price they pay. Without dedication they couldn't even complete their medical degrees, nor could they actually *continue* to practice medicine. Don't lightly dismiss this. Appreciating them will help you. It certainly does me.

Second, when you go to a physician recognize you are both human, he's just better trained than you are in bringing better health care. He is not your enemy. Don't bawl him out over trifles or merely because you don't feel good. He is an emotional being as you are. You are human too. That is what he has to work with. Your humanness. You can help yourself by helping him.

Doctors will tell you they don't know everything about medicine, about cures, or about you. They don't know exactly how you may react to their treatment. You may react like some other person, or you may not.

You are a unique person and so is the doctor. Work together for a cure.

Sure, some medicines may be better than others and they are seeking every day to make them better. Who gave them power to discover them? To improve them? Who provided the raw materials in His universe? GOD. That says something very special to you: don't wind up on the wrong side of God by being mean with your doctor and after seeking his help, by rejecting the best efforts he knows to help you medically.

I suggest you have a personal physician. Get to know him or her the best you can. Doctors want to help you. They want to help you as much, if not more, than you want to be helped.

In this, they reflect the nature of God who wishes you to *be in health* (3 John 2).

Speaking personally, I have been in the hospital four different times and each time I have experienced tender and loving care—the very best these dedicated people had to offer from the hospital staff, the nurses, and the doctors. Also, in these experiences there was always a close bond developed in which we all knew God is the ultimate Source of health. With all my calling to pray for the healing of people, I am keenly aware Jesus knew what He was talking about when He said, "They that are sick need a physician" (Luke 5:31).

Unfortunately, when I grew up I didn't learn to go to a dentist early. Dentists, however, have helped me save my teeth so that I have better gums and teeth than ever. I am very punctual in going to my dentist a minimum of twice a year. I even had an experience in a dentist's chair when the dentist and I prayed over a tooth that was not responding to treatment. Through his help and our prayer, my tooth was saved. I appreciate that.

A good professional relationship with your physician or dentist is often worth more than you can ever pay. It is an integral part of God's wonderful delivery system of health for you and your family. Despite flaws, mistakes, failures, it's a *healing gift* that I intend to have when I need it, both preventive and curative.

DO MEDICINE AND HEALING PRAYERS BELONG TOGETHER?

Some think because I had a healing of tuberculosis and am called to pray for the sick that I think medicine and prayer don't mix. That's foolishness. I've never divided them. Physicians and surgeons and dentists have helped me and my family so often, and I must say the same about healing prayers, that I combine them with the greatest of joy and warmest appreciation. I thank God I have BOTH. I also know that in praying for many physicians, or members of their families, I have encountered their warmest appreciation.

I personally know many physicians and dentists who are at home with both medicine and healing prayers, and the number is growing.

I hate to see a religious fanatic or a medical fanatic; I like to see Jesus *yoke* them together in a common goal of caring in His kingdom of love, salvation, and health — that's where they belong for our good.

I've dealt with many people in the medical profession and it is my observation that they (as a whole) are receiving the charismatic experience of the Holy Spirit more readily than others with whom I deal. St.

Luke, the medical doctor who was a traveling companion of St. Paul, was so interested in healings by faith that he was a co-worker with the great apostle. It is also Doctor Luke who tells us more about the work of the Holy Spirit and miracles than any other New Testament writer.

The prayer language when interpreted brings the tongue of understanding, as well as a deeper compassion, and can be very meaningful to a practicing medical person. Also, I think medical people sense their limitations. Many of them know they need a divine dimension in their practice.

The reason I believe the staffing of the ORU medical and dental schools has gone so well is because of this one point: highly competent medical and clinical educators on receiving the Holy Spirit, want to see a charismatic school of medicine from which ALL GOD'S HEALING POWER CAN BE TAUGHT AND CARRIED TO THE ENDS OF THE EARTH.

I, of course, continue to pray for the healing of people by the thousands. My deep appreciation for Jesus' statement, "They that are sick need a physician" (Luke 5:31), does not preclude me from God's words, "The prayer of faith shall save the sick, and the Lord shall raise [them] up; and if [they] have committed sins, they shall be forgiven [them]" (James 5:15).

Best of all, I see Jesus using the physician, the dentist, and persons who pray for the miraculous intervention of His healing power. It's just great to be an instrument of God in whatever way He chooses to use us. The important thing is the help that people get. Their better health is God's own wish (3 John 2).

SUGGESTIONS ON HOW AND WHEN TO GO TO A DOCTOR

The Lord's healing for our bodies and lives is one of the truly magnificent proofs of His personal concern in everything that touches our lives. His healing power stands out as one of the great love forces of all time. It is the outstretched hand of God. It is the thought of God revealed in miraculous action toward you and me. I love the healing power of Jesus Christ. And you and I need His healing touch!

The great healing power of Jesus Christ is readily available to us. We can't see it any more than we can see the wind. We can *hear* the wind. We can *feel* the wind. But we cannot see the wind. We can feel the great healing power of God. We can experience it. But we cannot really *explain* it to anybody.

Many people want me to explain my ministry of healing, to tell them why I pray for the sick, and they say, "How can this particular disease be healed by prayer?"

Well, in the first place, there are many different delivery systems for healing, all of them given to us by God in His truly great love for us all.

Our physicians are skilled. Their skill is of divine origin. Their skill has been made obtainable by a good God. We need dedicated doctors, and we need to call them when we're ill. We need to pay more attention to what they do and say in our behalf.

THE MISSING LINK

But, what else do we do? Because if that is all we do, then in most instances we can never fully recover. The Bible supplies the rest of the missing link. The Bible gives us the answer for the total healing of our spirit, mind, and body.

In that great book written by the apostle James in the New Testament, he says, *"Is any sick among you? Let him pray."* Then it says, *"Let him call for the elders of the church* (spiritual leaders of the church); *and let them pray over him . . . And the prayer of faith shall save the sick, and the Lord shall raise him up"* (James 5:13-15).

Notice the steps God has given us for the Lord's healing to enter our bodies.

1. CALL FOR HELP

This includes medical care. Jesus said, *"They that are sick need a physician." Let him call for his physician.* Let him call for prayer.

2. PRAY

Second, the Bible says, *"Let him pray"* (James 5:13). 5:13).

The Bible says that when you're ill, *you* should pray. During that time the study of the Bible is a part of your prayer. I know when I suffer any form of illness that I inevitably wind up reading my Bible. I often take it to bed with me. Sometimes I have it very near me while I try to sleep. I have enormous confidence in the therapy of Bible reading, of searching the Scripture, and of reading certain passages out loud to myself. I have sometimes read a specific passage, such as the 23rd Psalm, as many as five times out loud to myself.

> *Let him pray. Let him read his Bible. Let him*
> *contemplate God and his own life. Let him*
> *think about himself, and let him meditate.*

3. CALL SPIRITUAL LEADERS TO PRAY

The Bible offers us this valuable step! *Let him call* . . . Let him call for the spiritual leaders of the church.

Now the church is central in our lives. It is the Body of Christ, and the person who ignores Christ's Church is ignoring the great fundamental healing force in our universe today. Some people who believe in prayer turn off doctors. They leave their physician out of their scheme of life. I have no quarrel with anyone along that line. But as for me and my house, I do not leave my physician out. He has a part to play in my family existence and in my own personal life.

While some will neglect their physician, others will neglect their minister. They turn away from the church. But God reminds us that He has placed both here. They are put here for our good. Our physician and our church—especially when we have access to spiritual leaders who have an understanding of the miraculous power of God's healing. I accept both prayer and medicine reverently.

Some time ago I became very ill with a kidney stone. If you've ever had this experience you know how painful it is. My wife Evelyn called the Abundant Life Prayer Group to pray for me. She also called our family doctor. He came and gave me a shot. Then he said, "Oral, I've treated you medically; now I want to pray for you." He laid his hands on me and prayed a simple short prayer, full of sincerity and faith.

In a couple of hours I was OK. Now I don't know if it was because of prayer or because of medication, or both. It doesn't matter ... I was well. To be honest, I don't make demands on God as to what delivery system He uses. If God wants to heal me through prayer, I accept it from Him. If He chooses to use a doctor as the instrument to bring healing to me, then I accept that. Or if it's a combination of both, I gratefully accept it. For the Source of all healing is GOD.

"Let him call for the elders," or the spiritual leaders.

Let him call ... Why am I emphasizing the calling so much? Because I have discovered thousands of people are out of touch with God ... out of touch with their church ... out of touch with their minister. They do not realize the enormous ability of the church of Jesus Christ to bring healing, not only to their souls but also to their minds and bodies as well.

Do you know the act of calling for prayer is an act of faith? It helps you release your faith. It becomes, in effect, a point of contact for the releasing of your faith. When you pick up your telephone and call your minister or a spiritual person in the church and say, "Will you pray for the healing of my body, or for a member of my family, or my friend?" you are making it an act of faith. When you sit down and write a letter to someone like myself: "Dear Brother Roberts, I have an illness. I am calling upon you for your prayer," you're doing what the Bible said to do: "Let him call for the spiritual leaders of the church, and let them pray over him ... the *prayer of faith.*"

I am one of the spiritual leaders sent forth by the Lord to pray for the healing of people today. Some of us in the church have been given this special calling. We feel a rapport with people who are ill. We have a feeling for them that some people do not have. That feeling was given to us by God, and as we carry on our ministry that feeling continues to increase.

Those of us who pray for the healing of your body cannot be negative or uncertain in our believing. We are to be dominate in our faith, positive in our belief that God is a healing God, that God wants to recover our physical bodies—yes, our total selves.

It is one thing to pray over the person, and another thing to pray the prayer of faith — to believe, to release your faith for healing.

I think I do this best when I pray until I reach an inner feeling of knowing—a knowing that I have truly prayed. I cannot heal, neither can anyone else heal, but I can reach a state of knowing in my spirit that my prayer has reached God and the possibility of a cure is in His hands to use whatever delivery system He chooses.

It's very important to me in my healing prayers for a person to have the inner knowing that it is now in God's good hands. That's when I know I have prayed the prayer of faith.

To see it working so effectively for so many is the most heartening thing in my life; for my prayer is for the healing of the whole person.

Now say with me what we are learning about having a personal physician and healing prayer for health:

1. Doctors are against sickness and for health.

2. Medicine and healing prayers belong together.

3. Jesus says I need a physician.

4. The prayer of faith still works today.

5. God's wish is for you and me to be "in health."

STEPS THE LORD HAS GIVEN FOR HIS HEALING TO ENTER MY BODY

6. I will call for help. Jesus said, "They that are whole need not a physician; but they that are sick" (Luke 5:31).

7. I will pray—the Bible says, "Let him pray..." (James 5:13).

8. I will call the spiritual leaders to pray (James 5:14) or make contact so prayer can be offered.

key issue:

God Uses Prayer And Physicians To Complete His Healing Love In Me

Chapter 9

WHEN THE DOCTORS SAY THERE IS NO HOPE AND PRAYER HAS APPARENTLY FAILED—HOW TO FACE THE FUTURE

key issue: **I Face The Future Knowing My Life Is In God's Good Hands**

A physician friend said to me, "Dr. Roberts, what do you say to a person who evidently is not going to get well? How do you prepare him for death?"

I said, "Doctor, let me turn your question around. I know you face the same problem when you have done all you can, including surgery, and the person doesn't get well—let me ask, what do you do?"

He said, "Well, one doesn't always know what to say except give the truth that in spite of exhausting all medical help we can give, the individual is not going to make it. Of course if it is an aged person we all know that his time is necessarily limited; it's the younger ones with whom we are most baffled. Frankly, although we feel very deeply, we don't always know what to say or do beyond the services we have rendered. This is why I am most interested in your response."

I said, "Well, doctor, the one thing I try to remember is to put everything in perspective; for example, the Bible teaches that it is appointed unto men once to die, but after this the judgment (Hebrews 9:27). So I know that everyone you treat, or everyone I pray for, and even those we never see, ultimately are going *to die*. Death is an appointment each of us is going to keep. This includes even those who have recovered through medicine or through prayer or through a combination of both. This includes you and me. Everyone is going to die whether he is sick or well. There is a time when death will come."

He said, "I understand, and from the theological point of view I can see that following this course could be very helpful. From the medical side we physicians often feel we know that despite our best efforts death is going to take over, but it's never easy for the patient and family or for us. More and more we are being very frank with the person and the loved ones. At least, we can assure them we have done all we can medically."

I said, "Do you ever see what you think is certain death turn out to be the opposite?"

He replied, "We get surprises, don't we? According to our best medical practice and judgment, some who are not supposed to recover, do; and some who are supposed to, don't. It's puzzling, to say the least."

I said, "From the very beginning of my ministry of healing in 1947, there have been times I have prayed for persons I felt would recover; some did and some did not. But I know that I am not God, only His instrument. My part is to pray, His is to make the final judgment."

He nodded. "Let's say you have a person who has had medical care and you are asked to pray for him, do you ask God to *comfort* him or to *heal* him?"

"That's a question I face every day," I replied. "I am constantly praying for the sick. I very definitely pray for healing instead of comfort. Now I must explain what I mean. I pray for healing because I believe it is God's purpose to make people well. However, I don't always know when a person is going to die, or shall we say, is going to meet his divine appointment — so I pray with all the faith I have just as you, as a physician, use all your skill to make the person well. There's always the chance, however slim the chances of recovery seem to be, that there will be a cure or a healing. I know I must fulfill myself and my calling by praying with all the compassion and faith I possess. Still, I know God is the final judge of the time of death.

"On the other hand, I recall cases where I prayed when I discerned the person was going to die."

The doctor said, "How do you discern this?"

I said, "It's difficult to explain, it's a knowing that comes in my heart. I think you physicians often feel this same intuitive power."

He said, "True, but when you feel it, how do you pray? Is it a prayer for comfort?"

I said, "I try to remember one thing about God. No matter what I feel, GOD CAN STEP IN SO THAT THE PERSON MAY STILL LIVE FOR A LONGER TIME. Therefore, if I pray only for comfort, then the person may lose that one thread of hope."

He said, "Isn't there a moment when you actually know the person is not going to live?"

I said, "Yes, sometimes there is. What I do then is to ask permission of the loved one or loved ones to be frank about it, to tell them there is a death-time and it's here, the person is going. Or if I am dealing directly with the individual, I say, 'There may be something in medicine left for you, or God may still intervene through prayer, but in my own spirit I sense your homegoing. And I want to pray with you in a very special way.'

"Then I offer to pray that the person will die without pain, without fear and anxiety, and that there will be a great peace in meeting our Lord."

The doctor asked, "Is this usually well received?"

"So far," I replied, "the ones I have dealt with in this manner believe I am a God-called man; they respect my deep feelings and my frankness. Most tell me they are grateful to know what the real situation is. I recall only a few negative responses."

He said, "I can see from a theological point of view your intuititon and frankness are helpful. From the medical view we also often know when death is near but I'm afraid our training—or our temperament—does not always equip us to deal as directly with the patient about his approaching death. One thing we assure him, however, is that we are doing all we can."

I replied, "When my time comes I want to be dealt with in the most frank manner. The ultimate aim of my life is to live with God, to live beyond death. Death holds no terrors for any believer who knows that he, after death, will immediately be with our Lord (2 Corinthians 5:8).

"Do people ever apparently look upon you as they sometimes seem to look upon doctors, as God?"

"Oh, yes," I replied. "But I can understand that. We are gifted people. That's not baggadocio, but fact. We wouldn't have lasted this long unless we had something to give."

"How do you handle this?"

"By being very frank. I tell them I cannot heal. I am an instrument only. God is the healer. In whatever we do to bring about healing, God must be central in our thoughts. He is the ultimate Source."

"Does that turn many off?"

"Not many. In the first place, I and they need to be told the truth. Also, if they get their eyes on me—or on you doctors—other than as an instrument, they are looking to the wrong source, and that's bad. Another thing I find important is the spirit in which I say I cannot heal, that only God can heal. If in saying I cannot heal, I dwell on that, both the person and I get lower in our spirit. If I say it, then immediately transfer our attention to God who can, and who wants us to be well, that UP spirit is contagious for both of us. I've had so much experience with God in praying for people, I know that healing can happen. It doesn't always happen but that doesn't deter me from knowing it can."

The doctor said, "Let me ask you a different kind of question: let's say a person has had medical care and you are asked to pray for him, does the fact he has been medically treated hinder your faith for him?"

"On the contrary. Many times when I was told the person refused medical care, I told him I didn't feel he had done what he could do. My faith seemingly is stronger when I know more depends on the prayer. I asked one person if he had done something for his illness. When he said no, I said, 'Don't you think you should do for yourself what you can do?' It helps me pray better when I know the person has had good medical care. I would think prayers would also aid the doctor in the treatment he gives. At least, that's been my experience."

He said, "Good point. But let me ask you this, do you think when prayer is offered that God should be asked to actually intervene?"

I replied, "Doctor, I notice you men and women in the medical profession cut through all the theological red tape and go for a cure. You even hurt people sometimes by certain types of treatment. Surgery can be traumatic but unless you cut the thing out, how are you going to get the healing process going? You are against disease; you are for a cure, for health, and I appreciate that. To specifically answer your question, yes, I ask God to actually intervene and give life."

I added, "One of the biggest criticisms I've ever received is that I don't stop and say, 'God, if this is Your will, heal this person.' I believe since we don't always know the death-time of a person, we should go after a full healing. That's why I say, 'O God, heal!' "

IS THIS A DANGER POINT?

He said, "Isn't there danger in that approach?"

I said, "No more than your rolling up your sleeves and going to work to get the person well. Still, I admit there may be some danger. But I see more danger in destroying the faith of the person by sowing doubt in his mind about God's will concerning his health and well-being. He's got to feel the positiveness of our faith in a good God. He's already down in his spirit; instinctively he wants to be well, and yet perhaps he hasn't heard a spiritual word that strengthens his capacity to respond to getting well. Any doubt contributed by the person praying only adds to the person's self-doubt. He must be brought to a point of releasing his faith."

He said, "Why do you say, releasing his faith? Does he have faith?"

I said, "He certainly does, or why would he have come to the doctor in the first place, or for prayer? He believes. And you personally know, I am sure, that if he comes to you with a believing attitude, you are much more effective in your treatment of him."

He said, "Oh, yes, that's certainly true. A cynical, doubting patient pretty well defeats even the best medicine."

I said, "I believe that's because we are a spirit and should respond first from our spirit with a strong desire to be well. Our spirit should tell our mind and body to get well. If I were a doctor I would wish for believing patients. In my own ministry I try to work with people who believe, otherwise I am pretty helpless."

I referred back to his question on comforting the sick. I said, "In a sense, when you treat a person or we pray for him, we are bringing comfort. That's doing something that he can hold on to. It's also comforting—and encouraging—when a smile is given, or a pat on the shoulder, or a gentle squeezing of the hand, or a well-chosen word, or just our presence for a few moments beside the individual. But I want to make it clear that that cannot be a substitute for medical treatment designed to cure him. And it certainly is not a substitute for a definite healing prayer."

A PERSONAL EXPERIENCE

We talked of a bout I had had a few years ago with kidney stones. I referred to this in the previous chapter but I elaborated on it while I talked with this doctor. I told him the pain was so sharp it nearly drove me out of my mind. Fortunately, the ORU campus doctor, a

Spirit-filled man of God, lived nearby and he came quickly and administered a shot. Then he said, "Brother Oral, may I pray for you?"

I murmured, "Please do."

He got up on the side of the bed on his knees, put his hand on my forehead and prayed for Jesus to bless the shot he had given me and to add to it His own divine healing touch. I fell asleep while he prayed. Two hours later I awakened, *well!*

I said, "I can't tell you if the shot did it, or his prayer did it, or if both were instrumental. I don't know. What I do know is that when the doctor added a prayer *with* his treatment, it helped me believe better."

He said, "This may surprise a lot of patients but I personally know many surgeons who never operate without first bowing their head and quietly praying for divine guidance."

I said, "I wish more people knew that, at least the type of person I deal with in prayer. Prayer is powerful in getting a person to relax and to expect something good."

As we talked on, I told the doctor of people writing me, saying:

"Oral Roberts, until I heard you on television, I didn't know God was remotely concerned about my health, or money problems, or my personal needs. I thought He only wanted me to go to church, read the Bible, and go to heaven when I die."

I told him I get lots of letters from people like this and I can't ignore their healing need. I said I must deal with it—because I care, I am concerned. This is in general what I tell them:

"You live in your body 24 hours a day and you will until you die. Your body is vitally important to your well-being.

"You think through your mind; God cares that it is a strong and sound mind, and He cares that you are able to pray through your mind with the understanding.

"You have money problems, bills, etc., all the time. God cares that you have money, and enough money to live a good life.

"When you leave out God's concern for the smallest detail or need of your life, it can contribute to your problems getting worse. It certainly negatively affects your getting well from illness."

Then I said to the doctor, "Experts talk much of functional diseases, the ones caused by stress, by emotional upheavals, by bad relationships, or by fear. *Well, I want to point out, based on long experience, that physical maladies also affect the mind and spirit. The body can throw off its hurts upon the mental and spiritual part of man too.*

"I think to more successfully deal with it, we must think of healing in terms of the whole person. Actually the treating of disease, if it could be separated from man, probably could be cured by medicine quite easily. But it is not disconnected, it is the person who has the illness. The foundation of healing as given by Jesus begins with the person. 'Thy faith,' He often said, 'hath made thee whole.' The *person* must be healed. Some say if cancer is cured, isn't the person cured? Not necessarily. I deal with persons all the time whose bodies have been cured but who are not whole themselves."

My doctor friend said he couldn't agree more. Then he came back to the original question about preparing people for death, referring specifically to terminally ill people.

I told him I was once one of those people. I could have died, but didn't. I faced the pain, the fear, the threat of leaving dear loved ones, the lying there day after day, waiting . . .

He said, "What are some of your ideas or experiences in helping people who no longer have hope through medicine, and for whom prayer has not worked either?" The following is, in essence, what I shared with him.

HOW TO FACE THE REST OF YOUR LIFE IF YOU APPEAR TO BE TERMINALLY ILL

First, how to face the problem of the time left:

This can be days, months, or even years. You may want to go quickly, or you may want to hold on to life as long as possible.

To some, the longer the time the harder it is to bear. They would rather go on to meet the Lord than suffer any longer. This was my personal experience when the doctors gave me up with tuberculosis. As a 17-year-old, and on my way to the state tuberculosis sanatorium, I didn't really want to face lying there in bed, languishing away day by day until . . . I wanted to die, get it over with. I had to face the months and perhaps several years of slow dying. It was horrible. I was so young, so full of desire and goals ahead.

The young Methodist pastor in whose church I had grown up in part of my early life, visited and prayed for me. At that time healing through prayer was not understood as well, or as widely accepted as it is today. Each time he ended his prayer by saying, "Son, be patient."

In that day when we had little knowledge of healing prayers, also when there were none of the so-called miracle drugs which are so highly effective now in treating tuberculosis, being patient meant resignation and that was contrary to my nature. I think I would have died long ago had I been patient, as my pastor had suggested. (I'm glad that more and more pastors are changing this approach to a more positive one.)

Fortunately, I had parents and a sister and a brother who believed not only in medicine but in healing through prayer. They believed. I was being treated medically with the best that was available. The medicine was in my body when I was carried to a revival meeting and prayed for and felt God's Spirit flowing through me, and almost instantly my lungs were opened up and I could breathe, my coughing stopped, and in a few months I was well! I have no way of knowing just how much help I received from medicine or the prayer, or a combination of both—for I had them all. All I know is that following the prayer for my healing I began to get well—and I did!

What if I hadn't been healed? I've asked myself that many times. Some apparently are not. I say *apparently* because we don't always know. I mean by that there is evidence, at least to me, that some I have prayed for were healed and still died almost immediately. Because following the prayer all pain had vanished, even the symptoms of the disease; there was an ease in their entire physical system, a peace and calm. Was it a healing just before the appointed death-time? I like to think so. That is certainly the way I would like to go under similar conditions.

I hate sickness. Like physicians and surgeons, I am against it. I am for health, for without well-being what are you?

A PERFECT OPERATION! YET THE PATIENT DIES

Another surgeon friend of mine told me of instances in his practice when the operation was perfect. The body responded exactly as hoped, and yet, abruptly, the patient died.

I asked him how he felt about it. He replied, "I felt great about the operation but terrible about the patient's death."

Then he told me that early in his practice such an experience almost drove him out of medical practice. He said, "I couldn't understand it. I had done everything possible and it was working. I actually felt a glow inside. I had been instrumental in saving a human life, which they taught us in medical school is of supreme value. I wanted that person to be well so badly that I poured my whole being into preparing him for surgery, for the surgery itself, and the postoperative care, even though I hadn't know him before his referral to me. I gave him everything I had. Still, I lost him. And there was no understandable reason."

I asked him what he said to the loved ones. He said, "I was so emotional I'm afraid I didn't give them much help."

"But you stayed in practice?"

"Yes, it is my training, my dedication—really as a Christian, my calling from God. I couldn't quit and respect myself."

"That's exactly the way I feel," I said. "I am called of God to pray for people, to give them my very best. It's thrilling to see miracles work but no one knows how it hurts when you pray, and seemingly the person is helped, but then he dies. Still, I have to obey God's calling on my life and pray for those who seek my prayers."

A CANCER CASE I PRAYED FOR

I once prayed for a young mother in the last stages of cancer. The family held on to every word of my prayer which was coming out of my heart. When I had finished they crowded around me. "Is she going to be healed?" I said, "Do you want it like I feel it?" "Yes, tell us."

I said, "My deepest feelings are that she will be released from pain but she will go."

"When? When?"

"I don't know. It feels soon, perhaps in days."

Taking my hand the husband and father thanked me and said, "Well, if she just doesn't suffer."

Recently, I was back in that area doing a television special when I met the husband again. He was glad to see me. He said, "I suppose you have wondered what happened to my wife?"

I said, "Yes, I hoped for the best."

He said, "It was exactly like you said. From the hour of your prayer she had no more pain. She was able to sit up, talk to us, take her meals. At times she was very joyful and gave us hope she might make it. Each time though she would lapse back, seemingly knowing she was going to die. There was a peace that came over me, and over the children until we could accept it. She died about three weeks later in her sleep. We remembered what you said because it happened as you told us it would."

After five years he had just remarried, a lovely Christian woman whom he said was a real mother to his children, and they were very happy.

WHEN NOT EVEN THE PAIN CEASES

In other cases there have been times when nothing seems to work in the time left, not even release from pain. Heavy medication was administered so that often the person was drowsy or unconscious. I have no quarrel with this for pain can become unbearable. The only question I ask is theological. If the person dies in a drugged state and is not right with God, what then? Who is there in the person's lucid moments to help him repent—if he has not done so—and prepare to meet God? This is something doctors and loved ones should consider. For life doesn't end at death.

Always when I pray for such an individual I minister to the soul, asking him to repeat the sinner's prayer, and ask Christ to come into his heart. I've seen a lot of conversions in situations like this. The heart is usually more tender towards God. I believe the conversion is genuine. Conversion can happen in an instant, even on a deathbed because God's mercy extends on and on.

Just recently, one of the ORU coaches and his wife told me of a woman, a dear friend, who had received a spiritual conversion, and even though she was aware death was near she was rejoicing in the love of her Savior. They said, "That makes it so much easier for us to bear, and also her family, if she should die soon."

Second, how to face the problem of informing the person:

In our evangelistic crusades people would bring a loved one who might be dying with a disease and ask me not to reveal what the disease was. I refused. I said, "I'd rather not pray if I have to leave your loved one in the dark."

I never saw any person who seemed to resent my telling him the diagnosis of the doctor. He seemed relieved. Sometimes he already knew. People seem to appreciate my frankness as well as my prayers. Some recovered, some did not. The important thing for me was to give my best to the sick person and to trust my Source.

LETTERS ARE POWERFUL

In letters I get from ill persons, not only are their words there but their deepest feelings as well. Their spirit comes through. Because a letter conveys such depths of a person's condition and needs, I usually am able to pick up what I ordinarily would in person. I write back very candidly and always include a prayer for healing. I also give them a point of contact to use as a handle for their faith to be released.

Whether I feel I can discern if the person will recover or not, I always pray for his healing. Why?

Ask any doctor. He goes right ahead and gives his best, regardless. He is *against* disease and *for* health and life. There's always the hope he will administer what will work, or that in some seemingly miraculous way the person will recover.

At no time do I feel it advisable for anyone to withhold vital information from a very ill person who writes me for prayer. In this way, I feel there is a better possibility of discovering how to pray with the fullest power of faith.

There is much to be learned. Thank God, I believe in the continuing revelation of God's healing processes. I am a candidate to learn more.

Third, how to face the problem of the loved one's loss:

Several years ago I preached the funeral of a dear old friend in Christ. His first wife had passed on years before and he had remarried—this time to a relatively young woman and a very devout Christian. We loved them dearly.

At his death when I finished my message and we reached the cemetery, the wife went to pieces. A very large crowd was present and I was attempting to complete the committal service when she screamed and cried and attracted the startled attention of everyone.

We all understood the grief but not the hysterics. You see, it dawned on her she had lost more than a husband. She had lost relationship with a family whose mother had been their father's first wife. She sensed that the warm place she had occupied had been taken and she would soon face a cold world.

She was terrified; she was breaking up the dignity that belonged to this man's life and memory, a man who as a Christian leader had strong influence with the great and small. When things got out of hand I stepped over to her, took her hands, and whispered, "We all love you. Be quiet now. Remember, God is with you."

She screamed louder. The Lord gave me a word of wisdom in the form of a question as I got her quiet again for a moment. "Are you still, even at the death of your beloved husband, a Christian?"

She said, "Yes, oh, yes."

I said, firmly and I hope gently, "Then as a Christian you must believe in the resurrection of him from the dead. You must also believe the Lord of the resurrection will take care of you."

It was nearly enough but not quite. She screamed again. This time I went the extra mile. "Listen, these people are here because they know he died in hope of a better life after death. I understand your fear of the unknown future, the fears you have of it. But you are making a spectacle of yourself and by your actions you are casting doubt on your Christian beliefs."

It was like the calm after a thunderstorm. "Yes," she said. "Yes, I must get control, I must remember I am a Christian, I must remember Christ is close to me still and He will take care of me."

I said, "He surely will and you can depend on it."

The service was completed on a quiet note of hope. Later, she told me she had been totally unaware of anyone but herself and thanked me for dealing firmly with her. Today is a new day for her, for as she says, "I have found new outlets for talents I didn't know I had."

To me, it is very important how a Christian conducts himself at a funeral. If we as Christians believe what we say we do, there is never any need to go into hysterics. Tears—of course. Tears have a healing power in themselves and you should let the tears flow freely.

But hysterics—never! We can know God will take care of us and our future. We can trust Him.

WITNESSING AT DEATH

A Christian is a Christian in life and in death, in high and low moments. The ancient patriarch in the Bible, the man Job, in facing his sufferings said, "Though [God] slay me, yet will I trust in him" (Job 13:15). That is the position of the child of God, in good and bad, he will serve God.

I personally feel death is a most perfect time to give a witness of our faith. It isn't easy, nothing of value is ever easy. The one dying, the loved ones so deeply touched, are in a special position to let the Living Christ shine through—and He will.

Fourth, the problem of what to do with oneself in a lingering illness:

A friend who has a terminal illness tells me he is on a medical formula that his doctor changes whenever a new proven drug emerges and it helps him through the long days and particularly the long nights.

He says he has become a member of a prayer group where he has received the charismatic experience, which constantly gives him strength for his inner man. Through tongues, or the prayer language of the Spirit, he pours out his inner being to God, interprets back to his understanding and so is able to pray with THE TONGUE OF UNDERSTANDING. He says he doesn't know what he would do without it.

And he mentions my books, such as the *Miracle of Seed-Faith* and *A Daily Guide to Miracles*, as being particularly helpful in that they inspire him to reach out to others in Seed-Faith, knowing he will receive in return as he has given. Also, my letters in answer to his. "Every now and then," he says, "after reading your letter I lay it on my body as a point of contact and warm healing sensations flow through me. I have not been cured but I am being sustained by the presence of Christ I feel in me."

Why isn't this man restored to health? He received good medical care, lots of love, and earnest believing prayers. But no cure. I suppose one of the very first questions I shall ask God when I see Him face to face is, "Lord, tell me why."

Fifth, how to face the possibility of a new possibility:

To some, the prospect of facing a new possibility may pose another problem. They may say: *I have been told so many times I can't get well that I've accepted it. Now don't bother me with a so-called new possibility that may leave me even more distressed.*

On the other hand, I think even more distress might be caused by one shutting out the remotest possibility of something new being discovered in medicine, or God working through the prayers of one He especially has gifted, or a combination of both. Putting myself in this person's position is not difficult, for I have been there. For me, the possibility of a new possibility is better than giving up. Even if the new possibility never comes, I am a stronger person by trying.

A MAN FACING A NEW POSSIBILITY

I recently prayed for a crash victim who nearly lost his life. In the hospital, lying in traction and pain, he found our Sunday morning television program talked right to him and that it brought God to his bedside. When I reached him he was ready. Before this moment my prayers probably would have been received but not with the openness required for full effect. We hit it just right, the prayers helping the injured leg in a tangible way. It did something else. The following morning pins were to be put in his hip and his apprehension was such that I knew the orthopedic surgeon would be hindered by the negative emotions involved. In the prayer I discerned this and told him to relax and trust His Source to guide the surgeon who is often a very necessary part of God's delivery system of health. With a deep sigh of relief he said, "I feel released of this horror in my mind, which I couldn't get out of me. Now it is gone and I know the doctor will be successful in the morning when he puts the pins in my hip."

I noticed he said, "I know." It's so important to know, to reach a knowing in your heart, for that is what faith is— a knowing inside. It helped him face the possibility of a new possibility. Really, the special technique to be used for his hip was a radical new breakthrough in surgery. It was indeed a new possibility. It had only been perfected as a surgical technique a short time before. For the kind of surgery he needed on his hip, it was important to him to be open to a new possibility; otherwise, he might have refused it, or not known it existed. "With God all things are possible" however the possible comes!

A PERSONAL TESTIMONY

In the winter of 1975 a respiratory problem developed in me. I thought it would leave soon but it stubbornly held on. Days later a medical diagnosis showed it could be permanent. It was so serious my entire ministry might cease. Frantic feelings swept through me. I was scared. Then I got mad at the devil. Evelyn, my darling wife, said, "Oral this is just another trick of the devil. He tried to kill you when you were 17, and many times since. I believe God has a way for you, don't you?"

It was important that she said, "I believe God has a way for you, don't you?"

In saying, "Don't you?" she sensed I needed to say, YES, I DO!

We did three things:

(1) Obtained good medical help which was lovingly given by Spirit-filled physician friends of ours.

(2) We took one of our little alabaster boxes of oil and anointed each other, touching the other's forehead with a drop of the oil, as in Bible days. We believed the healing we asked for each other would come back to us. This is the Seed-Faith prayer in which you plant a seed for a miracle harvest.

(3) Before this time, I had realized that God's time had come to build a School of Medicine at Oral Roberts University. Now I felt I should plant the first seed with some funds I had, and of some I would trust Him to bring into my hand. *A leaping response* toward God for the medical school came into my heart. And in a way that I can't explain, *a knowing* came into my inner being that God would multiply

this seed back to me in the form of wholeness for my respiratory system. I went to
bed with this problem, wheezing and hurting, and finally into fitful sleep. When
I awakened the sun was shining into the
bedroom. I heard the birds chirping. I
got up, showered, shaved, and dressed. I
sat down to breakfast, humming a tune.

Suddenly I discovered I was breathing normally. I
was open all the way down. No pain, no wheezing. It
was delightful.

Evelyn noticed the look on my face. "Praise God," I
said. "Honey, I am restored, I am healed!"

We decided to keep a record of the miracles from
that seed of faith which she had joined me in planting.
Her Seed-Faith was giving the royalties of her new
book, *His Darling Wife, Evelyn* (in bookstores across
America), to the new medical school. In the first 60 days
we had 18 miracles, large and small, that we knew of,
including the restoration to full health of my respiratory
system. If I had all the money in the world and had used
it to have this healing, I would have gladly done so.
Planting a seed from the small sums I had, and Evelyn
giving her royalties as her seed of faith, opened me up to
receive my healing. This is another reminder from God
to me of the miracle of Seed-Faith, which is something
we do and something God does, through which needs
are met.

Still, I ask the question, when the physicians and the
prayers have not gotten through, what do you do then? I
feel compelled by the Holy Spirit to remind you there is
always the possibility of A NEW POSSIBILITY! Particularly if you keep yourself open to it.

WHAT TO DO WHEN YOU ARE TERMINALLY ILL

There is one other thing I feel is so important I am devoting the entire next chapter to it—THE RESURRECTION!

WHAT I CAN DO WHEN THE DOCTORS SAY THERE IS NO HOPE... AND PRAYER HAS APPARENTLY FAILED... HERE'S HOW TO FACE THE FUTURE

1. I know that death is a divine appointment (Hebrews (9:27).

2. I know God is the final judge of the time of death—still, I can remember that no matter what I feel GOD CAN STEP IN SO THAT I MAY STILL LIVE LONGER.

3. The ultimate aim of my life is to live with God, to live beyond death. Death holds no terrors for the believer, for after death he will immediately be with the Lord (2 Corinthians 5:8).

HOW, EVEN THOUGH THEY SAY YOU ARE TERMINALLY ILL, YOU CAN FACE THE REST OF YOUR LIFE... OR YOUR LOVED ONES

4. Know beyond a shadow of a doubt that Christ lives in your heart. Call for a min-

ister or a born-again Christian whom you have confidence in, and ask him to direct you through the Scriptures and then pray the sinner's prayer: O Lord, be merciful to me a sinner."

5. Be frank. Ask to know the truth about your case or the case of your loved one. This way you can better prepare.

6. Should you lose a loved one, of course you will feel the grief of the loss, so let the tears flow—they are healing. Then remember the resurrection and know God will take care of the future. We can trust Him.

7. Always remember that new and improved methods are being discovered every day. This hope will help to sustain you.

8. Being a Christian and praying in the spirit and with the understanding also helps sustain you.

9. Remember that there is always the possibility of a new possibility.

 key issue: *I Face The Future Knowing My Life Is In God's Good Hands*

Chapter 10

THE DAY WHEN YOU WILL BE TOTALLY HEALED

 key issue: **The Resurrection Is God's Perfect And Ultimate Healing**

Christ our Lord has one other healing instrument, the most powerful, the ultimate cure.

What is it?

THE RESURRECTION, THE ULTIMATE HEALING OF YOUR TOTAL BEING

The Resurrection!

I thrill at every healing act of God. To me, all healing is divine. Your salvation by faith in the death and resurrection of Jesus Christ. Your deliverance from fear, from frustration, and inner conflicts. The supplying of your financial needs. Your body getting well or even better, your sense of great well-being. Your entrance into miracle-living through Seed-Faith. Your guidance into a career which is right for you. Your use of the prayer language of the Spirit to help you pray better and to better receive God's response through your spirit to your mind. All these, and more, are part of God's healing power for you. Some come from medical help and care, some from prayer and faith, some from love, some from proper exercise, some from using good judgment—but all come from cooperating with the life forces God has put here for our better health and miracle-living.

There is a time, however, when none of these instruments work any further to prolong our physical existence on earth. Not the best medicine or surgery or exercise or counseling or prayer or faith—you are going to die. All of us are.

"It is appointed unto men once to die, but after this the judgment" (Hebrews 9:27).

CONVERSATION WITH A YOUNG COUPLE

A young couple, parents of three small children, who are very close to me in helping bring people into a greater faith for better health and miracle-living, said to me, "We have seen many healings, even things we believe are miracles. Still, people die, don't they?"

Before I could reply the young wife said, "You know, death is something we don't talk about; we don't seem to realize there is death. We are so young we don't encounter death often. But we think we and everybody should realize we are going to die."

I said, "Yes, and not become morbid about it, or not go to pieces when everything we know to do ultimately does not prevent death. Death is an appointment we shall all keep, whether we are sick or well."

I told them I was writing this book and was on the chapter of:

> When the doctors say there is no
> hope, and prayer has apparently
> failed, how to face the future.

He said, "Oh, that's very needed. What are some of the things you say?"

I related some of the things on this subject, then I said, "One thing we must keep foremost in our thinking and believing is—the resurrection."

He said, "Yes, we believe in the resurrection but how does that relate to the healing of sickness?"

I said, "It relates in every way because whatever the doctor misses, or prayer misses, or any other healing instrument misses, the resurrection WILL GET!"

"That's wonderful," he said. "But how?"

"Because the Resurrection is a Person, the Person of our Savior and Lord Jesus Christ who told us He is the Resurrection and the Life (John 11:25). The Resurrection is not a thing, it is our Risen Lord waiting to give us the fullness of life, to restore everything which has diminished us, including our bodies, in any way. It's complete healing, it's immortality, it's whole-man life made eternal, it's life after death in the same way that Christ lives in His glorified body."

My young friends almost shouted when they said, "Super! Super!"

Turning to each other they said, "I'm glad I'm a Christian, aren't you?"

I said, "To be a vital Christian is the greatest thing in the world. We serve a MAN who is the only One who says that we shall rise from the dead for He says, 'Because I live, you shall live also' " (John 14:19).

THIS IS WHAT SUSTAINED ST. PAUL

I believe the Bible with all my being. To me, it is the Word of God and it speaks God's life to me daily. It's also the explanation of life here and after death, and what to do about it. It is the only book that does that.

The man who wrote half of our New Testament, St. Paul, really opens up the healing and restorative powers that come through the resurrection.

It sustained him when
> he was stoned and left for dead,
> held in filthy prisons,
> shipwrecked several times,
> beaten, striped, scarred,
> persecuted until he despaired of his life,
> hit with weariness and pain often,
> left in hunger and thirst,
> sometimes cold and without proper clothes for warmth.

It sustained him when
> Satan's messenger struck him with a thorn in his flesh,
> he was forsaken by closest friends,
> he was lied on, spit on, called unfit to live,
> when he labored so hard that no one equaled him,
> when his prayers were not always granted or answered the way he asked,
> when his vision was so clouded it was like seeing through a darkened glass,
> when he had fears within and without, and in the midst of all these deadly negative forces working against him, he had the care of the new churches upon him . . .

His greatest hope is expressed like this: "That I may know him, and the power of his resurrection" (Philippians 3:10). And it is my hope too.

I like Paul very much because there is a lot he faced that I relate to, and so can you . . .

THE BELIEFS OF ST. PAUL THAT WILL HELP YOU

First, he believed whatever happened TO him he could bear as long as he knew he had God's grace.

When the satanic messenger bore in on his flesh with opposition like a thorn sticking into his body, and he prayed three times for God to remove it and God did not, he stood up to it until God spoke in his heart, "[Paul,] my grace is sufficient for thee: for my strength is made perfect in weakness" (2 Corinthians 12:9).

It was then that he knew God's grace was strong enough to see him through even the thorny messenger of Satan and he could relax, knowing he could win. It was then he knew nothing could defeat his spirit. Nothing could break his hold on his faith in God, or God's in him. Nothing earthly or satanic could put him down and keep him down. Such is the power of knowing you have God's grace in your heart, your life.

I have seen many people hit by bad things and have seen them go to pieces and never recover. And when I see this, I am reminded that not one of these people had God's sustaining grace in a knowable way, or if he did, he didn't rely upon it as having any power to sustain him.

The way I use this on myself when my opposition makes me reel and stagger until I feel like giving up, is to remember that God is all-powerful. God is in me, and I am in Him. His grace is real in my life. I am not alone. *God is with me. ME.* I get very personal about it.

While I am not going to relate all the bad things which have happened to me — and still do — I will say that my ministry of healing has been very controversial. I have made many mistakes and have been the cause of some just and unjust criticism and opposition. On the other hand, the junk and filth in some people's minds that they have thrown at me from every side has been enough to sour me on life or to wipe me out completely. But I am still here. The ministry is stronger than ever. More people are getting help through us as an instrument of God's healing power than ever before. Thousands, even millions. It is a wonder of God, in my eyes.

The overall sustaining power that has kept me steady, and kept me going with a good attitude and positive faith, is the grace of God I feel in my heart. His grace that makes me know God loves me, God believes in me, God is with me. In my weakness, and even my mistakes, He becomes more real to me as we walk together.

Second, Paul was the strongest in Seed-Faith living of any man I know.

It is Paul alone of all the New Testament writers who urges us to remember the words of the Lord Jesus, how He said, *"It is more blessed to give than to receive"* (Acts 20:35).

Better to give because only what one gives, not what is received, is multiplied back, as Jesus said in Luke 6:38, "Give, and it shall be given unto you."

It is Paul who said of the Lord, *God loveth a cheerful giver* (2 Corinthians 9:7), meaning you can only get into God's deepest love when you start making your love an act of voluntary, joyous giving. Wanting to give until you just can't wait to do it.

It is Paul who takes us back to God's eternal law of sowing and reaping that goes back to Genesis 8:22 where the Creator said, "While the earth remaineth, seedtime and havest . . . shall not cease."

Paul referred to this as the eternal Seed-Faith principle upon which a person's successful living is based. Sowing, then reaping, is a matter of life itself. With it, one succeeds; without it, one's life is a failure.

Paul said of this eternal law of God, *He which soweth sparingly shall reap also sparingly; and he which soweth bountifully shall reap also bountifully* (2 Corinthians 9:6).

Notice, Paul refers to "He which soweth..." This is you and me as persons, you and I are the sow-ers. We are also the reapers. And we sow OR reap either sparingly or bountifully.

Sparing, or scanty sowing produces a scanty harvest—the miracle is too small.

Bountiful sowing produces a full harvest—the miracle big enough to meet all your need (Philippians 4:19). That is tremendous to know *all* your need can be met when you *sow bountifully.*

It is Paul who said every man is to give, he is to give with purpose of heart, starting with his spirit—his inner self—not grudgingly or with arm twisting—or of necessity (meaning to give only because someone has a need of help) but to give because you have a purpose for it (2 Corinthians 9:7). It's the same as Jesus teaching you to give because you have a NEED. You have a need to GIVE and you give out of your need, as Jesus said the widow did, "She gave of her want," or need (Mark 12:44).

It was Paul who said if you give everything and don't do it with love—your giving will profit you nothing; you are like one throwing something infinitely valuable away (1 Corinthians 13), but if you give with love, the profit back to you will be of inestimable worth.

It was Paul who was the only New Testament writer to speak of *giving AND receiving*, as being inextricably woven together, inseparably linked, working together in a perfect whole.

"No church communicated with me as concerning giving and receiving, but ye only" (Philippians 4:15), Paul said.

GIVING and RECEIVING, he says, belong together.

He added, *"Not because I desire a gift: but fruit* (or harvest) *that may abound to your account"* (Philippians 4:17).

Paul said givers had an account with God which they can draw on and the return will be very large—it will abound to you!

You give first, and receiving will follow as day follows night. As you breathe out you breathe in, so as you give you will receive.

It was Paul who said, *"But my God* shall supply all your need according to his riches in glory by Christ Jesus" (Philippians 4:19).

No other New Testament writer used those strong unequivocable words. Why? I believe it was because Paul had such tough experiences that he had to learn the way into God's richer grace and God's sure way of giving back to him so he could sustain his life abundantly to the very end—to death itself!

I believe this with my whole being. I stake my life on it. Oral Roberts practices giving cheerfully and giving first. Oral Roberts practices making God his Source, the Source of his total supply. Oral Roberts expects to receive from his giving; he expects a miracle, many miracles, miracle-living.

I got it from the Bible but especially through Paul as he got it from Jesus.

Listen to this. Paul's Seed-Faith living gave him God's strength made perfect. By planting the seed first he uprooted

> the weeds of hate coming at him,
> the weeds of envy, jealousy, malice,
> bitterness,
> every kind of deadly negative emotion.

Paul planted

> the seed of love when hated,
> the seed of respect when disrespected,
> the seed of giving when not given to,
> the seed of approval when disapproved.

He gave concern, care, compassion, healing. And it made him strong.

Do you know how strong it made him? A man attacked so viciously that he was left for dead, yet was able to rise up, facing life at its meanest and death at its bitterest, and say:

> *"I have fought a good fight,*
> *I have finished my course,*
> *I have kept the faith:*
> *Henceforth there is laid up for me*
> *a crown ... which the Lord ... shall give me*
> *at that day: and not to me only ... "*

(2 Timothy 4:7,8).

Friend, you can say what Paul said as you get into Seed-Faith, which is putting the seeds in first. Then you have the resurrection already begun in you and its fullness to look forward to knowing the resurrection ultimately will restore and complete you as a full human being.

The fight Paul waged was a good one—there was no hate or bitterness or envy or murder in his heart. He fought c-l-e-a-n! And when the fight was over he was still a clean man.

Paul kept his faith in God. That is a miracle in the day he lived in, as it is in ours. Every corruption we face was rampant in Paul's path. The devil was as much the devil then as he is now, so was the messenger of the devil sent to harass and hurt Paul. They shook him, stomped him, and left him for dead. But the Christ living in him, in the unlimited power of the Holy Spirit, could not be shaken or stomped and left dead. Christ standing up in the shaken and stomped and left-for-dead Paul, gave him of His strength so that Paul was also able to stand up, his faith intact, his believing strong and unabated, his inner knowing as strong as heaven itself.

Paul finished his course.

He had a course God set him on, just as God has one for your life and for mine.

That course was to serve God, to share Christ with others, to plant seeds of his love in people's lives—to do it in good times and bad, when it was easy and when it was hard—and he did it. He did it.

THE FACT OF THE RESURRECTION

Always ahead of Paul was the fact of the resurrection. It beckoned him on. He knew that Jesus had given His life on the cross as the "seed of David," and as a seed he planted for all men—he knew that seed burst into harvest, and that harvest was the greatest miracle of all—the Resurrection. First, the resurrection of the "seed of the woman" promised by God in Genesis 3:15 and the resurrection of Jesus' own life as a seed.

Paul knew that the resurrection was his too—mine, yours, and for all those who live in Christ Jesus.

It was the fact of the resurrection shining like the noonday sun before Paul that made death palatable to him, that took away its sting, making it a grand passage from this earthly plane to the heavenly plane where there is no more sickness, no more pain, no more lack, no more tears, no more death (Revelation 7:16, 17).

The seeds I, Oral Roberts, am planting are not for nothing. Already, every day God is multiplying them back and my life is counting for Him. Every seed multiplied helps replenish my spirit. It helps my body too. Also, it helps my finances. It's a direct and personal foretaste and forerunner of the resurrection I shall have following the death of the body I live in.

I have a good fight to engage in.

I have God's faith in my heart to keep intact
    and active.

I have a course, God's plan for my life, to
    complete, little by little, day by day.

I have a crown laid up for me—it's there
    waiting.

Christ in my life makes my life worthwhile.

Christ in me makes my death worthwhile too. It is my death which will be swallowed up in VICTORY BY THE RESURRECTION. It will be your victory too, the greatest you will ever know.

Now, say to yourself with total confidence:

THE ULTIMATE HEALING OF MY TOTAL BEING IS THE RESURRECTION

1. I will always remember that whatever the doctor misses, or prayer misses, or any other healing instrument misses, THE RESURRECTION WILL GET. I WILL BE WHOLE IN MY GLORIFIED BODY.

2. I will believe, like St. Paul, that whatever happens to me I can bear it as long as I know I have God's grace in my life.

3. I will believe, like St. Paul, that sowing and reaping is a matter of life itself. If I sow sparingly I will reap sparingly—but if I sow bountifully, I shall reap bountifully. So I will plant many good seeds in this life.

4. Like St. Paul, I will keep my faith in God and finish my course, knowing there is a crown laid up for me and DEATH WILL BE SWALLOWED UP IN VICTORY.

key issue: *The Resurrection Is God's Perfect And Ultimate Healing*

A SUMMARY OF STEP NUMBER THREE...

Things I Must Do To Remember My New Relationship With Myself

key issue: 1. I AM USING MY INBORN ABILITY TO BELIEVE AND TO EXERCISE MY FAITH TO GET WELL AND STAY WELL. *I am learning to love and accept myself so I will be His servant and live in a state of better health and success.*

key issue: 2. I VALUE EVERY INSTRUMENT OF HEALING, AND LOVE THE SOURCE OF IT ALL— GOD. *Because I make God my Source I can expect Him to open up the proper instrument through which to work His healing wonders in me.*

key issue: 3. I KNOW JESUS RECOGNIZES MY HUMANITY AND WANTS TO HEAL ME BECAUSE I AM AN IMPORTANT PERSON. *I will have a positive attitude toward life and divine health, whether it comes from doctors,* *medication, or prayers, and will keep my eyes on Jesus, my Source.*

key issue:

4. **ALL SICKNESS IS FROM THE DEVIL . . . ALL HEALING IS FROM GOD – I AM BELIEVING GOD FOR HIS BEST.** *God is not a tyrant. He is a God of love. He loves me and wants me to live abundantly and be whole in every area of my being.*

key issue:

5. **I WILL NOT "FAKE IT" ABOUT MY ILLNESS – I WILL "FAITH IT" THROUGH TO HEALING.** *God loves me enough to give me healing even when I have given up.*

key issue:

6. **I HAVE A "FAITH MIRACLE" IN ME EVERY SECOND AND I WILL ACCEPT IT.** *I can learn to be more like Jesus was while He was on earth in human skin – I can have health too.*

key issue:

7. **I AM LOOKING FOR NEW DIMENSIONS FOR MY FAITH AND LOVE TO SHINE THROUGH TO OTHERS.** *In-*

stead of responding to deadly negative emotions, I will look for new dimensions for my love and faith to shine through to others.

key issue: 8. **GOD USES PRAYER AND PHYSICIANS TO COMPLETE HIS HEALING LOVE IN ME.** *I will look to every delivery system of His healing love. I will appreciate my doctor and pray for God to use Him as an instrument of His healing love for me. I will also make contact with the spiritual leaders of the church to pray, as stated in James 5:14.*

key issue: 9. **I FACE THE FUTURE KNOWING MY LIFE IS IN GOD'S GOOD HANDS.** *As I do all I know to do, God will do what is best for me.*

key issue: 10. **THE RESURRECTION IS GOD'S PERFECT AND ULTIMATE HEALING.** *I am alive. I will live in the resurrection. I shall be totally healed and alive forever and ever! I am God's property. I belong to God now and eternally!*

Dear Friend,

My prayer for you is that 3 MOST IMPORTANT STEPS TO YOUR BETTER HEALTH AND MIRACLE LIVING will help you learn that God is greater than any problem you have. But, I want to go beyond that. I want to pray for you personally. So, I invite you to write me and tell me your prayer request. I promise I'll pray and I'll write you back. Simply address your letter:

Oral Roberts
Tulsa, Oklahoma 74171

If you have a special prayer request, you are encouraged to call the Abundant Life Prayer Group at (918-492-7777). Call anytime, day or night, and a trained prayer partner will answer your call and pray with you.

Oral Roberts